The MacKennas of Truagh

The MacKennas of Truagh

—Revised Edition—

C. *Eugene Swezey, III*

HERITAGE BOOKS
2011

HERITAGE BOOKS
AN IMPRINT OF HERITAGE BOOKS, INC.

Books, CDs, and more—Worldwide

For our listing of thousands of titles see our website
at
www.HeritageBooks.com

Published 2011 by
HERITAGE BOOKS, INC.
Publishing Division
100 Railroad Ave. #104
Westminster, Maryland 21157

International Standard Book Numbers
Paperbound: 978-1-55613-849-2
Clothbound: 978-0-7884-8844-3

Also by C. Eugene Swezey, III:

The Swezeys of Huntington (1969)

The MacKennas of Trough (1971)

The Irish Chiefs: A Directory (1974)

The MacKennas of Truagh, Second Edition (1977)

Supplement to The MacKennas of Truagh (1980)

The Park Avenue Dairy Farm (1983) (With C.E. Swezey, II)

In progress:

The Swezey Family in America

Dedicated

to

My mother, Muriel McKenna Swezey,
a proud daughter of the celebrated
MacKennas of Truagh

CONTENTS

ILLUSTRATIONS

THE ANCIENT MACKENNA HERALDIC DESIGN

This design and variations of it appear on many gravestones in the Barony of Truagh and in surrounding counties. For further illustrations see Appendix B MacKenna Heraldry and pages 6a, 6b and 50a.

Coat of Arms: A deer being chased by two hounds, a mounted hunter and two crescents

Crest: A deer

War Cry: Cirtle Bharraigh Abu! (The tuft of tow to victory)

Plant Badge: A tuft of tow

Truagh was a flax growing district. The line or fine fibers were used for linen, whereas the tow or course fibers were used for cord, twine, coarse yarns and even as thatch for roofs. The abundance of tow may account for its use as a plant badge by the MacKennas. It has also been suggested that the MacKennas may have worn a linen kirtle or tunic and that:

> Possibly the Saxons of the Pale, whose doublets were of cloth, derided the girdled shirts, which formed the Irish male attire, calling it 'a woman's kirtle of tow,' and that the Clan MacKenna adopted the sobriquet and gave it back with death-dealing blows to their enemies.

> "Battle Cries of Irish Clans" from *Fragmentary Notes on Irish History*, State Paper Office, London. Cited in MacKenna, V. I, p. 258.

Flax Flower With a Twist of Tow

FOREWORD TO THE FIRST EDITION

The purpose of this study is to survey and describe the history of the family of MacKenna of Trough. It is hoped that such a study will help to interest MacKennas of today in their own clan and the history of it. To the knowledge of this writer there is no history of the MacKennas available at this time. This is not an unusual thing, for there are hundreds of Irish families without printed histories. In fact, the lack of interest by many people of Irish descent in their history may be due to the fact that there are no family narratives obtainable in attractive and reasonably-priced formats! This lack of interest has been pointed out by Mullin who says, "It is rather remarkable, considering our close links with Scotland, that the growth of clan societies, which is a feature of the Scottish scene, has had little or no counterpart in Ireland."

This history is, of necessity, brief and sketchy due to the difficulty of writing a history of an Irish family with only the rather scanty materials available here in America. I hope that some MacKenna in Ireland

will be motivated to take advantage of the primary source
materials there in order to write a truly comprehensive
history of such an ancient and distinguished family!

Grateful acknowledgement is made to all those who
helped to make this study possible. I am indebted to
the staffs of the American Irish Historical Society and
the Local History and Genealogy Section of the New York
Public Library. Also to the notes of Mrs. Ella MacKenna
Mielziner entitled "Some MacKenna Pedigrees," which she
intended to use as the basis for a history of the Clan
Kenna. These notes were compiled in 1944 but, unfortunately, Mrs. Mielziner didn't get the opportunity to
complete her project. She mentions a Philip MacKenna
of Corrella, Dublin, who had compiled a great deal of
MacKenna material. Mr. MacKenna is now deceased and I have
no idea what happened to his records!

In the mass of details that make up a study of this
type, some errors and omissions are inevitable. I can
only say that none were intended and corrections will be
made if they are discovered.

I had the good fortune to visit Trough in the summer
of 1964. It is a beautiful district with its gently
rolling hills and its many clear blue loughs. Much has
been said in poetry and song about the famous green woods
of Trough, but little remains today of their former glory.

With Niall MacKenna, may I say:

    Mo Mhile Slan Duitse Sios a Thriucha!

(A Thousand Healths to Thee Down at Truagh)

Huntington, New York   C.E.S. III

1971

FOREWORD TO THE SECOND EDITION

In the six years since the first edition appeared additional data has been gathered on the MacKennas, enough to justify a new edition of the history. The most obvious change in this new edition is in the spelling of the patrimony of the MacKennas, the barony of Truagh, Co. Monaghan. "Truagh" is the preferred spelling, so the spelling "Trough," used in the first edition, has been dropped. The Rev. Seosamh Ó Dufaigh says: "In fact neither spelling reflects either the local pronunciation or the original Gaelic meaning of the word. A pity Triucha or even Triuch (pronounced as one syllable) could not be revived."*

For the sake of consistency, the surname has been spelled in its full form "MacKenna" throughout the second edition. "McKenna" and "M'Kenna" and "MacKenna" mean the same thing, that is, the son of Kenna, mac being the Gaelic word for "son."

Since 1971 several authors have contributed signi-ficantly to the corpus of MacKenna history. Mr. Anthony Mathews has produced a very fine history published in

---

*Rev. Seosamh O Dufaigh. "Notes on the MacKennas of Truagh," Clogher Record, 1974, p. 221.

1972. His history, <u>Origin of the MacKennas</u>, is available from Heraldic Artists, Trinity Street, Dublin. And two excellent articles have appeared in the <u>Clogher Record</u>, the journal of the Clogher Historical Society. These are "Notes on the MacKennas of Truagh" by Rev. Seosamh Ó Dufaigh, (1974), and "The MacKenna Clergy" by Rev. P. Ó Gallachair, (1976).*

I recommend that anyone interested in MacKenna history and in the counties of Monaghan, Tyrone, Fermanagh, Cavan and Donegal should join the Clogher Historical Society. The annual membership fee is ₤2 or $5. Members receive the excellent annual journal of the society, the <u>Clogher Record</u>. Write to Miss Teresa McGrenaghan, Registrar, Clogher Historical Society, 15K Cornagrade Road, Enniskillen, Co. Fermanagh, Northern Ireland.

Anyone researching the MacKennas owes a great debt to the Very Rev. James Edward Canon MacKenna, who published <u>The Parishes of Clogher</u> in 1920. I would also like to thank the following who helped to make this edition possible: Mrs. Martin Leet, Jr., of Minneapolis, Minnesota, and Mr. Thomas MacKenna of Emyvale, Co. Monaghan, for photographs of the MacKenna country; to Mr. Martin MacCabe, Monaghan County Librarian, for texts of songs and poems; to Mrs. Mary MacKenna of Kilrudden House, Clogher, Co.

---

*Rev. O Gallachair's continuing article appears in each issue of the <u>Clogher Record</u> and is entitled, "Clogherici, A Dictionary of the Catholic Clergy of the Diocese of Clogher (1535-1835)."

Tyrone, for the text of "MacKenna's Farewell" (by the way, her excellent guesthouse is highly recommended and is right in the heart of the MacKenna country); the Rev. Sean Sweeney, and Mr. Michael Ó Curráoin for translating documents from Gaelic into English; to Mrs. Ruth Very, Mrs. Barbara Gray and Mr. Manol Dhimitri for translating documents from French and Spanish into English; Señor and Señora Pedro Undurraga of Santiago, Chile, for information on the Mackennas of Chile and for a copy of La Vida del Jeneral Juan Mackenna (Señora Undurraga is Fanny Mackenna y Lazcano, a direct descendant of General Don Juan Mackenna); Mr. Finbar McCormick for illustrations of the MacKenna gravestones from Donagh Cemetery and for permission to include the drawings in this history; Mr. Thomas Del Signore who did the sketches of places in Truagh; Mr. Hans Birk who did the MacKenna coat of arms in the frontispiece; Mr. Michael J.P. Gorman for his rendering of the ancient MacKenna coat of arms and Mr. George Hancox, who proofread the manuscript, and to the following for information and guidance: Rev. Seosamh Ó Dufaigh, C.C. of Enniskillen, Rt. Rev. L. Marron, P.P., V.G. of Carrickmacross, Dr. G.A. Hayes-McCoy of University College, Galway, Mr. Patrick P. Farrelly of Dublin and Seymour Leslie, Esq., of Castle Leslie, Glaslough, Co. Monaghan.

The librarians and archivists at the following
institutions provided invaluable information: the
National Library of Ireland, the Genealogical Office at
Dublin Castle, the Irish Genealogical Research Society
in London, the Archivo Historico Nacional in Madrid,
and the Archives Nationales and Bibliotheque Nationale
in Paris.

1977   C.E.S. III

FOREWORD TO REVISED EDITION

It is gratifying that there is enough demand for this book
to make another printing necessary! This revised edition is the
2nd. edition of 1977 with the 1980 supplement. I have taken
this opportunity to make some minor changes in the text and one
major change in regard to the coat of arms in the frontispiece.
I have come to the conclusion that the coat of arms with the
three lions' faces, which is often attributed to the MacKennas,
is not an authentic MacKenna coat of arms. There is no record
of this design in the official records in Dublin or at the
College of Arms in London. The design of the three lions' faces
originally appeared in the 19th century publication, *Burke's
General Armory*, a work considered unreliable in regard to
questions of armorial authenticity.

Rather than continue to perpetuate a bogus design I decided
it would be better to emphasize an heraldic design that has
great antiquity in its association with the MacKennas of Truagh.
I speak of the ancient 'hunt' design that appears on numerous
gravestones in Truagh and surrounding counties and,
interestingly enough, has been used by MacKennas in Spain and
Chile as an heraldic design! This 'hunt' scene alludes to the
ancient deer chase that first brought the MacKennas to north
Monaghan from their early home in Meath. I regret that my
inclusion of the shield with the three lions' faces in the 1977
edition of my book may have led people to purchase heraldic
items with that design on them.

Cirtle Bharraigh Abu!

C.E.S., III

Spring 1992

THE CENÉL FIACHACH MIC NÉILL

The MacKennas belonged anciently to the Uí Néill or
Clan Neill. The descendants of Niall of the Nine Hostages,
High King of Ireland from A.D. 379-405, took the clan-name
of Uí Néill and were divided into two great branches
called the northern and southern Uí Néill. The chief
clans of the northern branch (Clann Neill an Tuaisceirt),
whose territory lay in the present counties of Tyrone,
Derry, Donegal, and the north of Sligo, were Cenél Eoghain,
Cenél Conaill and Cenél Cairbre. Those of the southern
branch (Clann Neill an Deisceirt), whose territory covered
the Diocese of Meath, were Clann Cholmain, Cenél Fiachach
and Fir Teathbha.

The MacKennas were of the Cenél Fiachach Mic Néill,
the race of Fiacha, son of Niall of the Nine Hostages.
The MacGeoghegans and the O'Molloys were also of the race
of Fiacha, and, therefore, related to the MacKennas.
The question of how the MacKennas of the southern Uí Néill
wound up controlling territory in the land of the northern
Uí Néill is explained in the following:

> One of the sons of Fiacha is said to have
> migrated to Oriel, and to have planted a colony
> there. He was named Tuathal an Tuaiscirt,
> "Tuathal of the North," but he also, through two

sons, left a numerous progeny in Meath. In the Ulster province Cenél Fiachach settled in Magh Lemhna, a district in the barony of Clogher in the county of Tyrone. Of this branch of Cenél Fiachach, the most important representatives in the sixteenth century were the MacKennas of Truagh, a powerful clan who possessed a whole Barony in the north of county Monaghan during the period mentioned. Their genealogies show this.[1]

Another explanation for the MacKenna presence in the north is much more romantic and has become a family tradition. This tradition involves Hugh MacKenna and a deer hunt which started in Trim and ended in the barony of Truagh in north County Monaghan:

> Being of a hunting party at Trim, a deer of uncommon size was roused and started in a northerly direction, and the result was a day's hunting of a very desperate character, but on the approach of night all the huntsmen and their dogs, save Hugh MacKenna and his two trusty hounds, abandoned the chase, but he still continued to follow the game through the night and all through the following day and night. On the second morning of the chase, he and his gallant horse and hounds, though sorely spent with toil, ran into the deer on a hill above the old church of Errigal, where MacKenna dispatched his hard won prize with his hunting knife. Consequently the hill and fort bear the name of Lis Kein (fort of the knife) or Liskenna. The deer in his arms represents the animal roused at Trim; the two dogs, his faithful hounds; the two moons represent the two nights during which he maintained the chase; and the figure on horseback represents the huntsman and his gallant steed.[2]

While in Truagh, MacKenna fell in love with the daughter of Treanor, the local chieftain. He decided to remain in Truagh: "Hearing that another branch of his family had, in his absence, usurped the government of his territory, he yielded to the persuasion of his father-in-law and made his home in Truagh."[3] Eventually the chiefship of Truagh passed to MacKenna and remained in the family until the end of the seventeenth century. The legend recounted above may have some basis in fact, for many of the gravestones in Truagh bear a coat of arms showing mounted men accompanied by deer hounds in pursuit of a deer! In addition, the coats of arms of Owen MacKenna and of MacKenna of Dublin both contain hounds chasing deer.

There are further illustrations of the movement of the family from Meath to Monaghan:

> King over the cantred of Cladach,
> Mac Cionaith ye have heard,
> A scion, though hearty, martial;
> He is a Meathian though an Oirghillian.[4]
>
> And (sure) all have heard that o'er Hy-Kenna reigns
> The brave Mac Kenna, Patron of the Priests,
> But few men know that though in Oriel now
> His great ancestor thither went from Meath.[5]
>
> Lord of Triucha Ceud Cladaigh
> Is MacKenna, as you have heard recorded,
> A tree, though it bends, is strong,
> He is from Meath, though now in Orgiall.[6]

The celebrated deer chase is supposed to have taken place in the eighth century, according to tradition. From that point to the present day, the MacKennas are considered a County Monaghan family.

3

THE SURNAME MAC CIONAOITH

The MacKennas may have originated in or near the
village of Rathenna or Rathkenny, Upper Slane, County
Meath. This place name is similar to the family surname, and the family has been referred to as the Clan
Enna. The ancient Gaelic form of the name is Mac Cionaoith,
meaning the son of Cionaoith. This Cionaoith, a chief
who lived in the tenth century, was the eponym or
namefather of the MacKennas.

The meaning of Cionaoith has not been determined to
the satisfaction of modern genealogists and historians.
There are several theories, the essence of which are:

Mac Cionaodha - the son of the man beloved of Aodh,
                the fire god.[7] From cion, g. ceana,
                m, affection, esteem

              - son of the fire-sprung one.[8]
                cinn (head or source), aodh (fire
                god, Hugh)

              - head Hugh, Niall MacKenna is refer-
                red to as being of the race of Hugh
                during the Rising of 1641.[9]

              - cin or gin (without), aoth (servile
                work); thus, without servile work

              - cionaodh (slow), ionach (dirk)

All of the above are based on the name of the ancient
Irish god of fire, Aodh or Aedh. This name is usually
anglicized as Hugh. Many MacKennas used a second patronymic

McHugh, O'Hugh, and McAghey, which later evolved into Hughes, according to Rushe in his History of Monaghan.[10]

As far as Christian or first names are concerned, certain ones were used by the MacKennas over the centuries. The most popular ones were; Turlough, Toole (Tole), Ardal, Ross, Dunlevy, Laughlin, Niall, Shane, and Patrick. Unfortunately many of these old names are no longer in use, but MacKennas seeing these names may be inspired to use them in naming their children. See Appendix for further lists of names popular amongst the MacKennas.

THE GREEN WOODS OF TRUAGH

Nowadays Truagh is referred to as the MacKenna Country or the Home of the MacKennas. Surveys extending back to the fifteenth and sixteenth centuries indicate that the MacKennas were outnumbered only by the MacMahons in County Monaghan. In 1879 "Truagh was, and it may be said still is, the country of the MacKennas, so common is the name at the present day."[11] Writing in the 1920's, Canon MacKenna*said, "Clan MacKenna has been so long and so prominently connected with the parish and barony of Truagh, that any account of the parish would be necessarily incomplete without some notice of the clan . . ."[12]

Going back in time, family tradition tells us that Truagh was occupied by the Treanors when Hugh MacKenna pursued the deer in the eighth century. In 1181 A.D. the Mac Murchadha (Murphy) of Muintear Birn, a kingdom to the east of Truagh in the Tynan-Caledon area, controlled northern Monaghan.[13] When the MacKennas actually gained control of Truagh is difficult to determine with the evidence available. We find, however, records from the thirteenth century which clearly indicate MacKenna hegemony over Truagh.

*Very Rev. James Edward Canon MacKenna. See page 74 for
 biographical entry.

HERE LYEth
THE BODY OF
Patt McKENNA
WHO DEPARTE^D
THIS LIFE
MARCH th 2
1769

HERE LYEth
THE BODY OF
IOHN M^cKENNA

Some   Mac KENNA   HEADSTONES

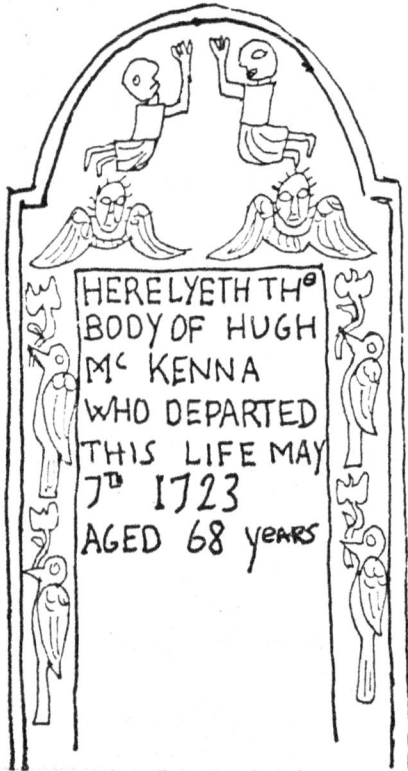

HERE LYETH THᵉ
BODY OF HUGH
Mᶜ KENNA
WHO DEPARTED
THIS LIFE MAY
7ᵈ 1723
AGED 68 years

CUM COPIASSPLENDOR

HERE LYETH
THE BODY OF
ROGER Mᶜ KENNᵃ
WHO DEPARTED
THIS LIFE MAY
THE 12 1740
AGED 35 YEARS

Truagh is the northernmost barony in County Monaghan. The original name was Triucha Ced an Chladaigh, meaning the thirty hundreds of Cladach. In the ancient Irish land measure a triucha ced, or barony, contained thirty ballibetaghs, each ballibetagh having about 960 acres. Another common land measure was the tate which consisted of 60 acres. There were 16 tates in a ballibetagh. In 1861 Truagh was surveyed and found to contain 37,376 statute acres.

Over the centuries Truagh has been called Truagh MacKenna, Hy-Kenna, and Trough. "Claddach, now the barony of Trough, County Monaghan is the patrimony of the Mac Cianaiths or Mac Kennas, who are still numerous there. They were of the race of Niall, settled in Meath."[14]

The barony of Truagh measures ten miles by eleven miles and is divided into two parishes by the river Mountain Water. The northern parish is known as Errigal Truagh, and the southern parish as Donagh. The parish of Donagh consists of 116 townlands covering an area of 16,010 acres. The old church at Donagh is in ruins and is surrounded by an ancient burying ground where there is a burial vault in which the MacKenna chiefs were buried. There are coats of arms on many of the headstones, which bear inscriptions from the seventeenth century. Nearby is the beautiful lake of Glaslough which has many ancient associations with the MacKennas:

7

The site of Glaslough was granted to O'Bear MacKenna by O'Nial of Ulster, on the conditions that he and his descendants should pay "Bonaghty" or tribute, and furnish white meat and oats to the Gallowglasses of O'Nial on certain days when they visited the holy well of Tubber Phadrick, near Glennan, and never to wage war with the O'Nials. This tribute was paid at stated periods in a house built of wood and osiers, at Anaghroe, or the Red River, now the seat of William Murdoch, Esq.[15]

St. Dymphna was said to be the Patron Saint of the district. She was believed to have conferred the virtue of preventing or curing almost all diseases on the waters of Tubber Phadrick.

The Chiefs of the Name, popularly styled "The MacKenna," lived in various spots in the parish of Donagh. "The eldest men in the barony state that his (The MacKenna's) house was situated near Glaslough."[16] Niall MacKenna, chief during the 1641 Rising, lived first at Tully Lough and then later at Portinaghy when his house was plundered. The last chief, Shane MacTool or Major John MacKenna, lived at Monmurry in 1689. The chiefs were variously referred to as Lords, Chiefs, and Princes of Truagh, and many of them were buried in the family vault at Donagh.

The parish of Errigal Truagh contains 153 townlands in the barony of Truagh and 14 townlands in the barony of Clogher in the neighboring county of Tyrone. The patrimony of the MacKennas consisted of the Barony of Truagh, Co. Monaghan, and the district of Portclare, Co. Tyrone. The total area is 24,792 statute acres. The Patron Saint of Errigal Truagh is St. Mellan (also called Mullin, Meallain, Muadan) and he is spoken of as Bishop of Airegal-Muadain. Apparently this was the original name of the area meaning the habitation of St. Muadan. The feast of St. Mellan is celebrated on August 30 and was in the past the occasion for visits to his well by large numbers of pilgrims. The well is located in the graveyard at Mullanacross: "The well is situated close to the north-east corner of the graveyard in the river bank opposite the gable of the former school-house. It is a constant spring of good pure water. I had it cleaned out and repaired, and it is in constant daily use. Originally it was lined with large stones and covered over in some way."[17] O'Donovan, writing in 1835, said that the well was not resorted to by pilgrims as it had been thirty years ago.[18]

The parish church is now in ruins, and Canon MacKenna comments on it:

> . . . where its picturesque, ivy-clad ruins, stand-
> ing in the ancient cemetery, amid the remains of
> generations of MacKennas, Treanors, Sweeneys,
> MacMeels and Connollys, cannot fail to recall to
> the student of the past, vivid memories of the
> Ages of Faith . . .[19]

The church fell into ruins before 1622, was rebuilt for Protestant worship, and used up to 1825. The most common names in the cemetery are MacKenna, Treanor, Connolly, MacGahey, Conlan, Slevin, MacCampbell, MacMeel, MacVicar and MacGeough.[20] A very interesting legend connected with this cemetery has been preserved in the ballad The Churchyard Bride written by William Carleton.

Many songs and stories have been written about the celebrated green woods of Truagh which, unfortunately, have fallen beneath the axe since the Middle Ages. The most famous of these is "The Green Woods of Truagh," an air composed by Niall MacKenna, a blind bard who died around the year 1700. Another indication of the extent of the green woods is the fact that the Irish word for wood enters into the composition of forty-nine names of townlands in the parish of Errigal Truagh.[21]

Writing in 1974, the Rev. Seosamh Ó Dufaigh said that ". . . the most common surname by far in the parish of Clogher today, as in Errigal Truagh, is that of MacKenna. Both parishes are the homeland of the MacKennas of Truagh."[22]

> During the long ages of persecution this clan displayed wonderful tenacity and perseverance in clinging to their ancestral home; and although members of it have figured prominently in the battlefields, the Council chambers, and the workshops of every country in the world, the clan held and still holds the place of pre-eminence in its native Truagh.[23]

THE OLD CEMETERY AT DONAGH

ERRIGAL CEMETERY AND
CHURCH (RUINS) AT
MULLANACROSS

THE MAC KENNAS AND THE MAC MAHONS

The MacMahons had been the rulers of Oirghialla (Oriel) since the thirteenth century. By the sixteenth century the boundaries of Oriel had been pushed back so that only the modern county of Monaghan remained in the hands of the MacMahons. In 1297 an agreement was made between Bishop Matthew MacCathassaigh and Brian MacMahon, King of Oriel and the nobles of Oriel. This agreement was a result of <u>Clericis</u> <u>Laicos</u>, the bull of Pope Boniface VIII in 1296, on church-state relations. Brian and the nobles of Oriel met the clergy at Lough Leck, the seat of the MacMahon chiefs. The agreement is of interest because it provides the names of the chiefs of Oriel and the names of their territories:[24]

        Brian MacMahon, King of Oriel
        Ralph MacMahon, Lord of Dartry
        Patrick O'Duffy, Chief of Teallach Gealagain
        Mahon MacMahon, Chief of Molfhinn
        Hugh MacKenna, Chief of Truagh
        Eachaidh MacDonnell, Chief of Clan Kelly
        MacMulrooney, Chief of his part of Clan Kelly
        Mahon, son of Giollachua, Lord of Crioch Mughdhorna
        Patrick MacMahon, Kinglet of Farney
        Walter O Carroll, Lord of Clan Carroll
        William MacMadagain, Chief of Clann Rothrach

By 1425 many things had changed, as is indicated in the following very interesting account of the relationship between the MacMahons, the MacKennas, the O'Connollys,

the O'Boylans, and the O'Duffys:

> The three principal chieftains of the
> Oirghialla in the time of Brian Mor, son
> of Ardghal, were O Buidhellan of Dartraighe,
> Mac Ceanaith in the Triucha and Duthach in
> Teallach Gealagain; and these chieftains are
> by right stewards of their own territories
> and O Connalaigh is the chief marshall of all
> Oirghialla.

> And at the inauguration of Mac Mahon each
> of these three chieftains receives either a
> rider's suit or forty marks of old silver in
> its stead. They and O Connalaigh and the
> comharba of Cluain Eois are the five lawful
> members of the council of Oirghialla.

> In return for every emolument we have enumerated
> above, they must bear a part of Mac Mahon's
> losses: every expense sustained by the terri-
> tory must be either paid for or levied by them,
> and each chief must provide a banquet for two
> full days each winter after Christmas, and
> O Connalaigh a banquet for one full day at
> Easter. At the inauguration O Connalaigh must
> supply the appropriate horse, the jerkin, the
> sword, the headdress, and the great spear -
> And it is not right to infringe on the terri-
> tory of an Oirghialla man at any time.

> The following is a part of the emolument which
> the chieftains of Oirghialla receive from
> Mac Mahon: Each chief gets a rider's suit
> from MacMahon and each chief's wife a suit of
> clothes from Mac Mahon's wife.

> It was Brian Mor who gave these emoluments
> and the chieftains increased their homage to
> Mac Mahon in return, an ounce of gold annually
> from each tate of land in their estate as a
> token of respect, and as a sign of his authority
> and their obedience. That is why the money is
> said to be due from those tuatha from that
> time until the time of Rudhraidhe, son of
> Ardghal. He is the man who remitted half of
> the rent in lieu of their stipend (i.e. the
> emoluments); the remaining half was to be
> continued to be levied on them by him and his
> posterity, etc.[25]

12

This very valuable account tells us not only who the important septs were in County Monaghan but also describes the way the territory of Oriel was administered by the MacMahons and the chiefs under them. The MacKennas appear to have owed nominal allegiance to the MacMahons and, as the years passed, "MacKenna was able to improve his position sufficiently to make overlordship as nominal as possible and alone among the minor chiefs of Monaghan he kept his independence until the end of the Gaelic era."[26]

FLAX

THE LORDS OF TRUAGH

The historical records indicate that the MacKennas,
like the other Irish septs, were busy consolidating and
defending their territory during the Middle Ages. There
are not many references to the MacKennas in this period,
perhaps because:

> Having been, like their progenitor,
> more addicted to peaceful domestic pursuits
> and to the pleasures of the chase, than to
> the field of battle, the clan has no very
> distinguished military achievements to its
> credit, and its records are stained with few
> deeds of violence. They had occasional domestic
> feuds, as every Irish clan had.[27]

In 1261, Philip MacCinaetha, chief of the Cantred,
was slain by Gilla-Muire Ua Cairre[28] and in 1325,
Donough MacKenna, Chief of Truagh, was slain in MacMahon's
church.[29] MacKenna was described as chief of the territory anciently called Triocha ched an Chladaigh. We can't
be sure what caused these murders, but in this same period,
"the first stone of the monastery of Louth was laid by
Donogh O'Carroll, (Donough O'Carroll, who died in 1169 A.D.,
was the last King of Oriel. In 1148 he assisted at the
opening of the new churches of Louth and Cnoc na Seangan),
lord of the territory, after defeating MacKenna of Triuch
who contended for the honour of its erection.[30]

The MacKennas became involved in the feuds of other septs as in 1434 when Owen O'Neill took the crannoge of Lough Leary from his sons, who were assisted by the Clan Kenna, or MacKennas of Truagh, in Oriel.[31] And again, in 1436, Niall, son of Owen O'Neill was slain by the Clan Kenna of Truagh, assisted by Henry O'Neill and the people of Oriel.[32]

On 17 March 1508, Philip Maguire of Fermanagh, apparently a guest of MacKenna of Truagh, was attacked in the church by Redmond Og MacMahon. Maguire was able to successfully resist the attack,[33] but his descendant, Conor Og, wasn't so fortunate. In 1576, Conor Og, son of Donough Maguire and some of the nobles of Fir-Luirg were slain in Truagh.[34]

Warfare was not confined to one sept against another. There was considerable fighting within septs for control of the chieftainry and of the territory. The Annals of Lough Ce describe the murder in 1402 of MacCinaith of the Triucha by his own brothers![35]

This does seem like a great deal of violence but, in comparison to many other families, perhaps less than the average. Nominal allegiance to the MacMahons meant that the MacKennas were drawn into many of the MacMahon feuds and into open battle with the English and other enemies of the MacMahons. It isn't always

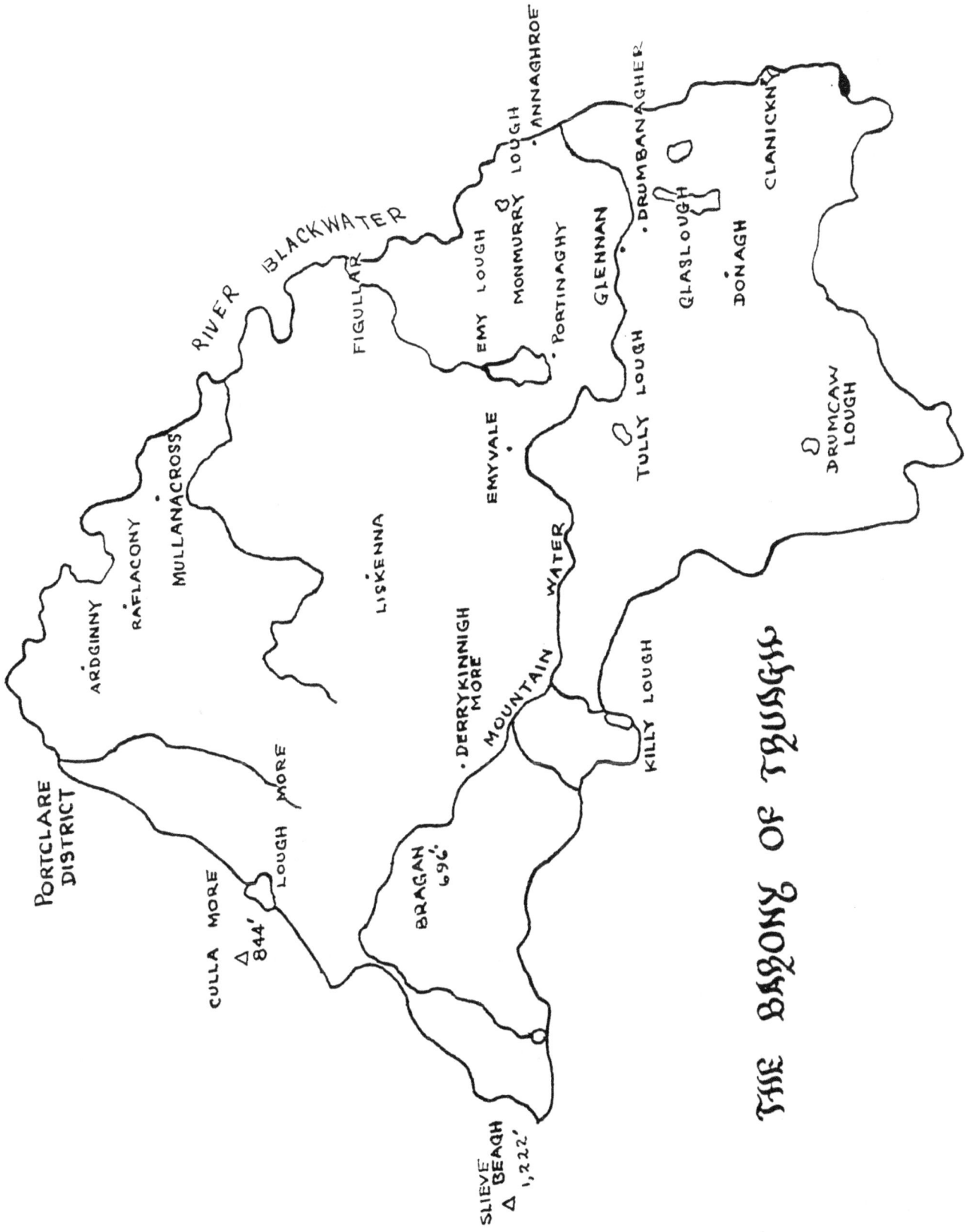

THE BARONY OF TRUAGH

PORTCLARE
DISTRICT

RIVER BLACKWATER

FIGULLAR

EMY LOUGH

MONMURRY LOUGH

ANNAGHROE

PORTINAGHY

GLENNAN

DRUMBANAGHER

CLANICKNA

GLASLOUGH

DONAGH

DRUMCAW LOUGH

ARDGINNY

RAFLACONY

MULLANACROSS

LISKENNA

EMYVALE

TULLY LOUGH

CULLA MORE
△ 844'

LOUGH MORE

DERRYKINNIGH MORE

MOUNTAIN WATER

KILLY LOUGH

BRAGAN
696'

SLIEVE
BEAGH
△ 1,222'

15a

clear as to whether the MacKennas supported the MacMahons consistently throughout the period. In 1496 a battle took place in the barony of Farney in Monaghan. On one side were the English, the O'Reillys, and the men of Dartrey and Farney, and on the other were the O'Donnells, the MacMahons, the O'Hanlons, and the MacKennas. The MacMahons and their allies won.[36]

In the 1530's the MacMahons were supporting the O'Neills against the English. There is no mention of MacKenna participation in these engagements, although MacKenna* says that "In the various expeditions of the clans of Oriel against the English of the Pale, the men of Truagh were among the first in the field and the last to quit it."[37] An interesting verse describes the MacKenna support of the MacMahons:

> Go muster the men in the greenwood,
> 'Neath the flag of Clan Mahon arrayed,
> And tell them the troops of MacKenna,
> Are hurrying to our aid.
> Quick! speed every man to the saddle,
> The foremost has entered the glen,
> And there rides the Chieftain MacKenna
> The first, in the front of his men.[38]

                              W. Collins

Wealth consisted of livestock before the plantations and confiscations of the seventeenth century. "In Ulster wealth consisted almost wholly in herds of cattle, which were driven from one place to another as pasture became exhausted, a practice known as creaghting."[39]
*Canon MacKenna

16

MacKenna*says that the area had fertile land and abundant cattle and grain and that it was wealthy and prosperous during this period.[40] He goes on to say that the people made nominal contribution to the chief for the support of his dignity and the maintenance of the government.

The chief of the MacKennas was chosen by the leading members of the sept according to the ancient Gaelic custom. Succession did not necessarily follow from father to son, for all those within a certain family group were eligible. The English custom of primogeniture, whereby succession went from father to eldest son, eventually came to replace the old system. The inauguration of a new chief was quite an elaborate and serious ceremony and took place at some sacred spot in the territory of the sept. According to the Irish custom, a chief is known simply by his surname; in fact, most of the members of the sept used only their Christian names, thus reserving the use of the surname for their chief. The chief of the MacKennas then, was simply known as MacKenna or The MacKenna.

Bishop MacKenna made an important comment on the question of the succession of chiefs:

> It may be no harm to note here in passing that to be able to trace one's descent from the Chief of the Clan at a given date is not a matter of such transcendent importance as some people seem to think. The Chieftain of the Clan did not go by inheritance from father to son, but by election from the members of the clan. Hence there are many families of the clan at all times of equal social standing as the chief for the time being.[41]

*Canon MacKenna

The MacKenna chiefs were known for their
hospitality. As MacKenna tells us, "Poets credit
the MacKenna clan with having been generous patrons
of the Church and the clergy, and with dispensing
lavish hospitality."[42]

SURRENDER AND RE-GRANT, VICTORY AND DEFEAT

Beginning with the sixteenth century, the history of Monaghan is largely one of strife and resistance to the English invaders. The conquest of Ireland had been going on for over four centuries, but was greatly intensified after the succession of Elizabeth to the throne of England. The MacMahons were a buffer against the English of the Pale, and the English took advantage of the feuds amongst the MacMahons. Behind the MacMahons were the O'Neills, who were fighting the English throughout this period. This meant that the MacMahons were right in the middle and had little choice but to take sides, trying to choose the side that would benefit them the most. The MacKennas, of course, were drawn into the personal feuds amongst the MacMahons and into the fighting between the English and their enemies. In 1569, for example, after the death of Shane O'Neill, the Act of Attainder mentions "the Troo called M'Kynors" as being forfeited.[43]

Elizabeth's policy in Ulster was to confiscate the lands of the native Irish and turn them over to English soldiers and adventurers. The first step was to divide

Ulster into shire ground, that is, into counties on the English model. Surveys began in 1585 and the report on Truagh revealed that, "MacKenna has a crannoge, as these wooden houses built on artificial islands are called, marked either on the lake of Glaslough or on that of Emylough, in the Parish of Donagh, in the Barony of Truagh."[44] MacKenna's home was probably in the lake of Glaslough as "There is no crannog that I know of in Truagh, except, probably, the island in Glaslough."[45]

Confiscation generally began after the surveys were completed, but in the case of County Monaghan a very different result occurred. On 12 April 1587, Sir Ross MacMahon agreed to surrender all the lands of Monaghan to the English and, in return, the lands would be regranted to him. Of course he didn't possess all of Monaghan, and the other chiefs of the county protested. The result was that the reigning chiefs agreed to sur- render their lands to the Queen who, in return, divided the land and regranted it to the MacMahons and the MacKennas. In this manner the chiefs avoided having their land confiscated and settled by the English. This agreement, known as the Settlement of 1591, took place on 10 September, 1591 and involved six MacMahons and one MacKenna. The seven chiefs received from 2,000 to 5,000 acres each and

20

TRUAGH

GLASLOUGH
•

MONAGHAN
MONAGHAN
•

• CLONES

DARTREE

CASTLEBLAYNEY •
CREMORNE

FARNEY

CARRICKMACROSS
•

THE BARONIES OF COUNTY MONAGHAN

were allowed rents from their freeholders amounting to ten pounds for every 960 acres, the chiefs to pay quit-rent to the Crown.

Patrick MacKenna, Chief of the Name, is described in the Act of Settlement as, "Mac Kenna a Chief Gent; and freeholder in the Barony of Troughe."[46] He was the chief of his sept and the greatest freeholder in the country at this time.[47] The act divided Truagh into 14 ballibetaghs and 12 tates. MacKenna received 3 ballibetaghs and 12 tates, amounting to about 3,600 acres for his demesne.* His two sons, Owen MacPatrick and Shane, received 5 ballibetaghs. The remaining acres went to freeholders under MacKenna (see Appendix E). He was required, ". . . to pay yearly to her majestie, seven shillings and sixpence for each tate of sixty acres (about 3 halfpence per acre) and to yield the turning out, for her majesty's service, of two horsemen and four footmen."[48]

	Irish Acres*	Rent Due	Rent Due From Tenants	Total Lands
*MacCionnaith of Truagh	3,600	₤22 10s	₤56 17s 6d	5,460 acres

* equals about 3 English acres

21

The act reveals a further erosion of the territory of The MacKenna. In the past the chiefs had controlled the entire barony of Truagh, but in the 1591 settlement MacKenna lost one-third, the Glaslough portion of the parish of Donagh, to Brian Og MacMahon. There was also a loss of authority, for restrictions were placed on his tenure of the land which were contrary to Gaelic custom. MacKenna was required to limit his will to his eldest son, Owen MacPatrick MacKenna, following the English custom of primogeniture. Later he avoided this restriction by dividing his estate before his death.

By following the policy of surrender and regrant, the MacMahons and MacKennas were able to hold onto their lands longer then many of the other Irish chiefs. Beneath the surface, however, the Monaghan chiefs had caused a fundamental change in the ancient Irish system, for:

> Under Gaelic law, a chief's right in the lands he ruled was a limited life-interest, and there was no succession by primogeniture; his surrender of lands was therefore, from the Irish standpoint, invalid, and to turn him into a tenant-in-chief of the crown was to ignore the rights of his clansmen.[49]

In 1591 an incident occurred which brought the MacKennas into the heat of the struggle with England. It was at this time that Hugh Roe O'Donnell escaped from his English captors at Dublin Castle. He was

accompanied by two sons of O'Neill, and the three began
their long journey through the snow to their homes in
the north. One O'Neill was lost in the snow and Art
O'Neill and Hugh Roe continued on despite suffering
from frostbite of the feet. MacKenna sent out a spirited
Gaelic welcome to O'Donnell:

The Truagh Welcome to O'Donnell

Shall a son of O'Donnell be cheerless and cold
　　While MacKenna's wide hearth has a faggot to spare?
While O'Donnell is poor, shall MacKenna have gold?
　　Or be clothed, while a limb of O'Donnell is bare?

While sickness and hunger thy sinews assail,
　　Shall MacKenna, unmoved, quaff his madder of mead?
On the haunch of a deer shall MacKenna regale,
　　While a chief of Tirconnel is fainting for food?

No; enter my dwelling, my feast thou shalt share;
　　on my pillow of rushes thy head shall recline.
And bold is the heart and the hand that will dare
　　To harm but one hair of a ringlet of thine.

Then come to my home, 'tis the home of a friend.
　　In the green woods of Truagh thou art safe from thy foes:
Six sons of MacKenna thy steps shall attend,
　　And their six sheathless skeans shall protect thy repose.

MacKenna, I., p. 253

It isn't known if O'Donnell took advantage of the
invitation, but MacKenna's welcome is certainly a good
example of the hospitality that the MacKennas were famous
for!

　　The escape of Red Hugh was a sign of what was to
come. Once again the Irish would have to make a choice
as to whether they would support each other, support the
English, or try to stay out of the trouble. The O'Neills

23

were the great power in the north and were determined
to gain the support of all their Irish neighbors by one
way or another. It was in 1592 that raids were made into
Monaghan from the surrounding counties. Great amounts
of wealth were carried off in these raids.

In July of 1592, while MacKenna was attending the
sessions at Monaghan, Con O'Neill, son of Hugh O'Neill
the Earl of Tyrone, raided MacKenna's country and carried
off great numbers of cattle into Tyrone. The cattle
were recovered, "But yet MacKenna stands in fear."[50]
The government called upon O'Neill for an explanation
and demanded that he deliver the men who had staged the
raid to be executed at Monaghan. MacKenna attempted to
stay out of the approaching trouble by supporting the
English. He was in league with Patrick MacArt Moyle
MacMahon, sheriff of the county and the Queen's MacMahon.
These two supplied information to the English concerning
a conspiracy by which the Earl of Tyrone, Maguire, and
some of the MacMahons of Monaghan swore to aid the
Spaniards when they landed in Ireland. MacKenna was
described in the deposition as, "One of the chiefest
men and of most force in that county."[51]

As indicated in the deposition, Maguire and Brian
MacHugh Og MacMahon (the last MacMahon lord in Monaghan)
were ". . . in trouble with the government and making

24

themselves very bad neighbors to such people as did not agree with them, especially to Connor Roe Maguire, Patrick MacArt Maol MacMahon, the MacArdles and MacKennas."[52] In September the English garrison at Monaghan was attacked and the English retaliated by gathering their allies-MacKenna, Patrick MacArt Moyle and Patrick Dubh MacCollo-and marching against the rebellious MacMahons. They advanced to Drumcaw and Roosky and destroyed the possessions of Brian MacHugh Og and his brother Rurai. Joining up with O'Neill, this army defeated Maguire near Belleek.[53] By October, 1593, all the chiefs of Monaghan were returned to their homes except for the traitors: Brian MacHugh Og and his brother Art MacRorie, and the three sons of Ever MacCoolie.[54]

Patrick MacKenna and Patrick MacArt Moyle MacMahon continued to support the English until the Battle of Clontibret in May of 1595. After this battle they abandoned the English cause and went over to O'Neill. They supported O'Neill throughout the remainder of the Nine Years' War (1593-1601). On 24 December 1595 Monaghan town was captured by the Irish, and the entire county was free of the English. The war reached its high point in 1598 with the victory of Hugh O'Neill over the English at the Battle of the Yellow Ford. The MacKennas fought under O'Neill at the Yellow Ford and the son of MacKenna, Patrick, a captain, was killed.[55]

25

GLASLOUGH FROM THE CASTLE LESLIE GARDEN

The brilliant victory of the Yellow Ford was short-lived, however, for the Irish suffered a disastrous defeat at Kinsale in 1601 which brought the war to an end. The MacMahons were present at Kinsale and, although there is no specific mention of the MacKennas, we can assume they were present also. Shortly after Kinsale, the English devastated Monaghan by their scorched earth policy. O'Donnell surrendered in December, 1602, and O'Neill made submission in March, 1603. The death of Queen Elizabeth six days before denied her the opportunity of seeing the Tudor conquest of Ireland completed. The English could afford to be generous to their conquered enemies and granted pardons to everyone involved. In effect the old Gaelic order had come to an end, for now the chiefs and the great leaders like O'Neill and O'Donnell had lost their authority to the government in London. Never adjusting to this situation, the two earls and about one hundred followers left Ireland in September 1607 for the continent of Europe in what has come to be known as "The Flight of the Earls."

THE RISING OF 1641

"The Flight of the Earls" brought a change in English policy toward Ireland. In 1603 James I succeeded Elizabeth as the English sovereign, and he began a policy of relative generosity to his conquered enemy. The action of the Irish earls in 1607, however, led to a new system of confiscation of lands followed by the plantation of English settlers. This time period, 1600-1641, saw the gradual erosion of the native land holdings, which would disappear almost completely by the early eighteenth century. Each rising was followed by confiscation and, even in times of peace, the Irish did not seem to be able to hold onto their lands.

In the Monaghan Inquisition of 1605, the church lands located in Greghlen and Grange were allotted to Thomas Ashe of Trim. MacKenna, meanwhile, in an attempt to avoid willing all his lands to his eldest son, had divided his estate in advance among his heirs. On 27 July 1607 he failed to pay his rents of ₤22, 10s to the government and, in consequence, his letters patent from Queen Elizabeth became void. He further encumbered the MacKenna patrimony by taking out mortgages on his lands. The Irish seemed unprepared for the more complex English society with its

legal system and its world of business. They were unable
to adjust to the change, and, "a new landed gentry, better
versed in business, law and the power of money, took
their place. The clan system lingered on, . . . only as
a sense of solidarity among its members, for its land,
its law and its leaders were gone."[56]

Of course, official English policy was to destroy
the Gaelic system through legislation as well as through
economics. The chiefs had "lived as independent rulers,
each of whom, to quote a sixteenth century writer, 'maketh
war and peace for himself . . . and obeyeth to no other
person, English or Irish, except only to such persons as
may subdue him by the sword.'"[57] In 1605, a proclamation
abolished the authority exercised by Irish chiefs and lords
over their tenants, and declared the tenants to be "the
free, natural, and immediate subjects of his majesty and
not the natives or natural followers of any lord or
chieftain whatsoever."[58] Other legislation did away
with the customs of tanistry, whereby a chief recognized
his successor before his death, and the custom of
gavelkind, whereby the lands of the deceased were divided
up among his relatives. All these further weakened the
old Gaelic system and insured English control over Ireland.

In 1608 the rising led by Sir Cahir O'Dougherty was
supported by the Monaghan chiefs. Brian Og MacMahon of

the Spear Handles (Brian Na Samhthach) was killed and his lands in Truagh were confiscated by the government. The Crown then granted these lands to Sir Thomas Ridgeway, thus giving the English a foothold in the barony of Truagh. Apparently the son of MacKenna actively supported O'Dougherty in this insurrection.

Losses of land continued, and on 20 August 1610, the Inquisition at Dungannon, Co. Tyrone, declared the ballibetagh of Portclare to be within the boundary of Co. Tyrone. MacKenna thus lost Portclare and its 960 acres (16 tates) which were granted to Sir Thomas Ridgeway. Problems with Portclare dated back to a feud that existed between the MacKennas and the O'Neills. The O'Neills claimed Portclare, even though the Lord Deputy had declared it to be part of the patrimony of The MacKenna.[59] In the 1606 re-settlement Portclare had been given to Patrick MacArt Moyle MacMahon. Eventually Portclare passed to the Erskines, who renamed it the Manor of Favour Royal. The original MacKenna possession of Portclare explains why it is still included in the parish of Errigal Truagh although it is actually located in Co. Tyrone. In 1611 Patrick MacKenna began the destruction of the green woods of Truagh by selling to Sir Thomas Ridgeway, "700 trees, 400 boards and planks, besides a great quantity of stone and timber for tenements, with timber for the setting up of a watermill."[60]

Not only was land lost by forfeiture and mortgages but also by outright sale. Apparently attracted by the offer of money, several MacKennas sold land during this period. In 1626 alone, Shane MacKenna sold five townlands to Thomas Blayney and Toole MacKenna sold three townlands to Bartholomew Brett. By 1640 there were sixteen MacKenna landed proprietors whose lands were greatly reduced in size, as compared with the situation in the Elizabethan agreement of 1591.

"The Forty One" was the natural outcome of the English confiscation and plantation of Irish lands. The leader of the rising in the north was Sir Phelim O'Neill, and among those who joined him were the "tall MacKennas from the song-famed woods of Truagh."* The chief of the MacKennas was Captain Niall MacKenna, and he was described as, "MacKenna of the Truagh, Esq., principal man of his sept."[61] Canon MacKenna says that Niall was a man of very quiet and retiring disposition."[62] Patrick MacKenna died about 1612/1614 and was succeeded as MacKenna by Niall, who was a minor. Niall was made a ward of the King under the protection of Sir Thomas Ridgeway. He was educated in the English religion and habits at Trinity College, Dublin, from age twelve to eighteen. Despite his education he adhered to his Irish background and was a prominent leader

---

*Mrs. J. Sadlier. The Confederate Chieftains: A Tale of the Irish Rebellion of 1641. N.Y.: Sadlier, 1860.

30

PORTINAGHY HOUSE

in Co. Monaghan during the rising. Niall had been appointed High Sheriff of Monaghan in 1638 and became a captain in the rising. The following MacKennas were out with their chief in 1642: Tole MacKenna, Shane Og MacKenna, James MacKenna, Brian Og MacKenna, Brian MacHugh MacKenna, Patrick MacD____ MacKenna, Gilgrome MacKenna and Phelimy MacKenna. Other Truagh landowners who supported him: William Field, Patrick MacMahon, James Balfe, Richard Phillips, Hugh MacShane Galt MacMahon, Hugh Mac-Gonnell, Brian MacRedmond MacGlasney MacMahon, Owen Mac-Redmon MacGlasney MacMahon, and Henry Cowell.[63]

The English didn't agree with Canon MacKenna's description of Niall, he was "so obscure as to my knowledge I never saw him," and "young and rude, though he was brought up to civility and learning, having been a ward of the King."[64] The English expected MacKenna to furnish to the outings of the county four foot soldiers and two horse, five swords, one pike, two lances and one culliver (rifle).[65]

The gathering of the Ulster clans is described in "The Muster of the North" by Gavan Duffy. The following stanza mentions the MacKennas:

Down from the sacred hills whereon a Saint communed with God,
Up from the vale where Bagnall's blood manured the reeking sod,
Out from the stately woods of Truagh, MacKenna's plundered home,
Like Malin's waves, as fierce and fast, our faithful clansmen come.

Fighting in Monaghan was particularly intense, and many atrocities were committed on both sides. Both members of Parliament from Monaghan, Richard Blayney and Nicholas Simpson, were killed in the fighting. Most of the English and Scottish settlers suffered considerable losses along with the native Irish. The first objective of the Irish was the capture of Monaghan town, which was accomplished by the MacKennas and their allies in 1641. Niall MacKenna and Turlough Og O'Neill captured Robert Berkeley and Nicholas Simpson and their homes. Berkeley and Simpson surrendered on the condition that MacKenna himself would agree to spare their lives. MacKenna carried out his promise even to the point of guarding the house for nine months against the fighting going on all around.[66] On 8 February 1641 a proclamation put a price of four hundred pounds on the head of Niall MacKenna. Anyone who killed MacKenna and brought his head to the lord's justices would receive the reward plus a pardon![67]

According to some accounts Shane Og MacKenna attacked and killed a great number of British Protestants after the repulse at Lisburn. Owen Roe MacKenna was accused of being a participant at the battle of Portadown bridge in 1641. These accounts were given to the British authorities by residents of Truagh. Apparently many such reports were given and collected during the rising and used as evidence against the rebels after their defeat.

On 23 October 1641 the MacQuaids* attacked Glaslough and seized all the arms and ammunition that they could find. On the same day, a little later, Turlough Og O'Neill took possession of the castle and removed all valuables. A week later, James MacTool MacKenna attacked Glaslough and confiscated the little that must have remained after the first two attacks! In March 1642:

> Information was given to the enemy that Sir Feidhlim would be in the camp of the MacMahons and the MacKennas on the afternoon of the 5th of March. A cavalry troop and a hundred infantry attacked the camp of the MacMahons. The latter opposed them for a while; however, Art Ruadh, son of Patrick, son of Art Moyle, was wounded and captured; and his brother Rory with several others of our men were killed. That happened beside Tullyallen (near Drogheda, Co. Louth).[68]

The rising in general had been going badly, so in July 1642, the northern chiefs met at Portinaghy, the home of MacKenna, to discuss their plans for the future. After some time they concluded "that everyone should shift for himself, since they were in no posture for defence; some intending for France, some for Spain, Flanders, etc.; others for the Highlands and the more remote parts of the kingdom."[69] A messenger appeared during the meeting and announced the good news that Owen Roe O'Neill had arrived in Ulster to take command of the army! Spirits were immediately raised, for Owen Roe was an experienced

---

*The MacQuaids were fosterers to Turlogh Og O'Neill, a brother of Sir Phelim O'Neill.

military commander and he would succeed his kinsman Sir
Phelim O'Neill and lead the Irish to their greatest
victory in the rising at the Battle of Benburb in 1646.

In the spring of 1643, the English under Sir Robert
Stewart invaded Truagh and captured the residence of
MacKenna (Baile MacKenna). Not satisfied with that, he
took as much booty as he could carry and kidnapped Mac-
Kenna's wife into the bargain! Another attack into

MacKenna's country followed:

> About two days after the unsuccessful
> rebel attack on Augher, Tyrone, some twenty
> horse, with Master Archibald Hamilton, a bold
> soldier, forraged into the county of Monaghan,
> where they encountered a strong party commanded
> by the great MacKenna which they encountered
> very fiercely and at last routed the rebel,
> killed one of his special commanders that had
> been a commander in Spaine, slew about
> thirty horsemen and twenty foot and recovered
> many of the British cattell.[70]

All of these attacks left Truagh in a very sad
state, as recorded in the following: "Towards the end
of the autumn (1644), after the corn had been scattered,
and destroyed, and trampled, some of the Creaghts returned
to the land, notably Niall MacKenna, of the race of Aodh,
to vigorous Truagh, and Turlough O'Neill, son of Brian,
to the Fews . . ."[71]

The Irish victory at Benburb in 1646 was the high
point for the Irish, and thereafter their fortunes
declined. Cromwell arrived in Ireland in 1649 and within

a year quickly and effectively reduced resistance throughout the country. The fighting was concluded in May 1652 by the Articles of Kilkenny. The Rising of 1641 was a failure and resulted in even greater confiscations and plantations. Thirty-four townlands were seized in Truagh from MacKenna and became government property (see Appendix F). On 12 August 1652, Niall MacKenna, Chief of his Name, was excluded from freedom for life and estate. His estate was confiscated, and he left Ireland in November 1653 to join the Spanish army. He appeared later in a Spanish document of 1687 as Don Nelano Maquiena, Lord of Truje (Truagh), Co. Monaghan (See Appendix M). It has been estimated that some 30,000 Irish soldiers were allowed to go into exile after the rising.

After confiscation, the lands of the Irish were then distributed among the British soldiers and adventurers who had helped to quell the rising. A census taken in 1659 is misleading - it lists 112 MacMahons, 91 MacKennas, 69 O'Duffys and 56 O'Connollys, as heads of families. The point is that they were fast becoming tenants on land that had formerly belonged to them. Hearth Money Rolls of 1663-1665 lists the following:

1.	MacMahon	158
2.	MacKenna	121
3.	O'Duffy	111
4.	O'Connolly	80
5.	MacCabe	50
6.	MacWard	41
7.	MacArdle	37
8.	MacIlmartin	36

72

MONMURRY HOUSE

MONMURRY LOUGH

35a

In the parish of Donagh there were 104 English Protestants and 198 Irish Catholics in 1659. In Errigal Truagh there were only 30 English Protestants and 300 Irish Catholics. The native Irish may have greatly outnumbered the English, but it was the English who owned and controlled the land. A look at the list of Donagh Landed Proprietors in 1640 found in the appendix will help to illustrate this point. By 1659 Mathew Ancketell had possession of all the land found on the list but for one tate, which was given to Coll Carey of Dublin.

The leaders of the Irish had disappeared, some finding a better life in foreign armies, and others slipping into a much lower level in the social order. As Mullin says, "It was the ordinary members of the clan, who have always had to struggle for existence, who survived as farmers and labourers on the land of their forefathers."[73]

One of the largest landowners was the Irish branch of the Leslie family. The late Sir Shane Leslie wrote, "I was brought up at Glaslough, in the county of Monaghan, in Ireland, on the townland of Castle Lesly - such space upon God's earth as previous Leslies had been able to hold by purchase, forfeiture, or force of arms against The MacKenna of Truagh."[74] This statement indicates the ways in which the native Irish lost their lands and also the desperate time the newcomers had in trying to hold onto it!

36

THE LAST CHIEF

Irish hopes rose again in 1685 when James II became the King of England. Many of the acts suppressing Catholics were suspended, Catholics were appointed to government offices, and regiments were recruited from among the Irish Catholics. The policies of James were not appreciated by many of the English, who decided to invite William of Orange and his wife Mary to become rulers of England. Upon the arrival of William in England, the Irish Catholics joined James II, and the Irish Protestants joined William. Thus began the Williamite War of 1689-1691. Significant battles were fought at Aughrim, and at the Boyne on 1 July 1690. The war ended with the seige of Limerick, after which several thousand Irish soldiers left to serve in the armies of France, Spain and Austria. Most of the continental European armies had Irish Brigades, which provided a haven for the defeated supporters of James II and the House of Stuart.

The MacKennas actively supported James II, and the chief, Shane MacTool MacKenna (also known as Major John MacKenna) was an officer in the army of James. An interesting account of MacKenna's activities occurred on

26 December 1688: "Captain Hovendon was one of those who, along with MacKenna, were to seize upon Charles Leslie - these instructions were contained in a letter in cypher to MacKenna, sent from Drogheda and signed by Fr. Garland and Fr. Daly."[75]

In 1689, James II appointed Shane MacTool MacKenna as High Sheriff of County Monaghan. This appointment led to the death of MacKenna and, ultimately, to the end of the MacKenna lordship in Truagh. The MacKenna met his death at the Battle of Drumbanagher on 13 March 1689. There are two versions of the battle, one by the Williamites and one by the Jacobites. According to the Williamites, the Protestant forces under the command of Captains Richardson, Coll and Anketell were on their way from Glaslough to Antrim. On their way they encountered a poorly armed force of Catholics at Drumbanagher. Drumbanagher contains a hill and rath and is located about one-half mile from Glaslough. Two troops of horse and one of infantry attacked the Catholic position. The Catholics wasted their ammunition in an effort to stop the charge and then had to resort to hand-to-hand combat. Captain Anketell was killed and Major MacKenna and his son were captured by the Protestant forces. MacKenna had been wounded in the encounter and was killed by his adversaries in revenge.[76]

In the Jacobite version, the Major was killed as a protest to his appointment as High Sheriff of the county. The anti-Catholic magistrates refused to recognize the appointment and issued a warrant for MacKenna's arrest. The Williamites surrounded the Major's home at Monmurry, about a mile from Glaslough, in order to arrest him. In the encounter several of MacKenna's retainers were killed and William Anketell was killed.[77] Which account is truthful is a question we probably shall never be able to answer. In any event we know that MacKenna was killed and, "some accuse the murderers of the further brutality of having, with mock ceremony, presented his bleeding head to his wife on the lawn of their residence!"[78] Canon MacKenna felt that the Jacobite version was a more probable account of the occurrence than the Williamite description.[79]

With MacKenna's death and the defeat of the sept at Drumbanagher, the MacKenna lordship over Truagh was destroyed for all time. Shane MacTool (Major John) was the last Lord of Truagh duly inaugurated by Gaelic law and custom. He was buried in the MacKenna vault at Donagh, where so many of the chiefs were buried over the centuries.

The events of the Williamite War led to the final collapse of the old Gaelic order in Ireland. The MacKennas, like other Irish Catholic families, were ruined by their adherence to the Stuart cause in the time of James II.

The remaining leaders of the family left Truagh for other parts of Ireland or joined the Wild Geese (na Geana Fiadhaine), as the soldiers who left Ireland to join foreign armies were called. The descendants of the Wild Geese remained in their adopted countries and generally continued in the military tradition of their ancestors. There were three Irish regiments in the Spanish army, two of which were commanded by MacKennas. Colonel John Joseph MacKenna led the Regiment of Ultonia, and Sir John MacKenna, Knight of Alcantara, was colonel of the Regiment of Hibernia. The most famous MacKenna in foreign military service was General Don Juan MacKenna, whose life is discussed in Appendix N.

After the death of Shane MacTool, his son and heir John MacKenna came into possession of the Truagh estate. He is listed as John MacKenna of Monmurry in "A List of County Monaghan Freeholders of 1692." He sold his patrimony in 1703 to James Moore of Aughnacloy and moved to County Longford. Early in the reign of Queen Anne, MacKenna returned to Truagh and obtained leases of some of the lands which had previously belonged to him. He obtained leases in Errigal Truagh from Anketell of Anketell Grove, and in the barony of Monaghan from Lucas of Castleshane and Lady Blayney. In 1746 John MacKenna died leaving his possessions to his four sons: Nugent, Francis, Felix (Phelim),

DRUMBANAGHER FORT

and William. He was buried in the ancient churchyard at Donagh with his ancestors. His will mentions not only the distribution of land but also such interesting items as beds, spoons, saltcellars and:

> I leave and bequeath unto my grandson
> Andrew MacKenna my black mare, both
> my shoe and knee buckles and the
> second best cow about the house.
>
> I leave and bequeath unto my sister
> Alice the Truagh cow.
>
> > Last Will and Testament of
> > John MacKenna of Corlost,
> > parish and county of Monaghan.
> > 24 April 1746

There has been a great deal of controversy about Shane MacTool MacKenna (Major John MacKenna). Philip Shirley, in his History of the County of Monaghan (1879), referred to MacKenna as the last of his line having been killed in the Battle of Drumbanagher in 1689. But this position was challenged by Denis Rushe in his History of Monaghan for Two Hundred Years (1921), who proved that MacKenna was not the last of his line, and that he did have descendants. Rushe's evidence was in the form of a Bill of Discovery filed in the Court of Exchequer on 18 Jan. 1749, and on five claims on petition to the Trustees at Chichester House in 1700.*

Another reference to MacKenna is found in O'Hart's Irish and Anglo-Irish Landed Gentry When Cromwell Came to Ireland, (1892):

---

*Margaret Falley. Irish and Scotch-Irish Ancestral Research: A Guide to the Genealogical Records, Methods and Sources in Ireland. Evanston, Ill. 1961, pp. 517-518.

Cromwell's soldiers murdered the Chief of Truagh and his five sons after sacking the place and setting it on fire. One of the Chief's sons, who was then a child at fosterage up in the mountains, escaped the massacre, and was afterwards The MacKenna (commonly called the "Major"), who in March, 1689, was killed defending the Fort of Drumbanagher, near Glaslough, for King James II: and who was buried in the family grave in Donough, parish of Donagh, County of Monaghan, and Diocese of Clogher.

I have never found any evidence to support the statement of O'Hart but insert it as an interesting reference to the last chief.

Drumbanagher Fort

PENAL LAWS AND THE RISING OF 1798

The eighteenth century was to be one of increased
repression and coercion. The Irish had lost in the
Williamite War and were not to be allowed to forget it.
A whole series of coercive measures were passed and which
have come to be known as The Penal Laws. These laws were
intended to deny Roman Catholics any part in the public
and political life of the country. These measures pre-
vented Catholics from holding public office, from owning
land, from voting, from education, and from entering
trades and professions. Perhaps even more serious in the
eyes of the Catholic population were the laws forbidding
the practice of the Catholic religion. Priests were
outlawed, churches were taken over by the government and
Catholics were forced to pay tithes to the established
church which they didn't even support! There were bounties
for the discovery of priests who were practicing their
religion and, if caught, they could be condemned to death
or transported to be sold as slaves.[80]

Throughout the eighteenth century the Irish continued
to resist English rule generally by what we now call
guerrilla warfare. One of the groups consisted of disbanded

soldiers from the army of James II and were known as rapparees. In 1722 Bryan MacOwen Og MacKenna, a rapparee, was captured by the English. In 1763, William, Niall, Owen, John, and Hugh MacKenna were charged with high treason for their support of the group known as the "Hearts of Steel." As Canon MacKenna said, "While members of the clan were fighting the battles of other peoples on the continent, others at home in Truagh continued to fight Ireland's battles."[81]

The century ended with the Rising of 1798, another futile attempt by the Irish to overthrow their conquerors. In Truagh itself, the Society of United Irishmen made many converts: "Practically every young man of standing and respectability, in the Barony of Truagh, was enrolled in the Society of United Irishmen."[82] Many of them joined the Monaghan Militia with the aim of gaining support for the cause of Irish independence. The authorities became alarmed at the success of the United Irishmen and decided to move the regiment to Blaris Moor outside Belfast. Here four of the most active United Irishmen were discovered and court-martialed. They were sentenced to be shot, but were offered pardons if they would inform on their associates. Two of the four were Owen and William MacKenna, sons of Owen MacKenna of Dheariagh. The father went to Belfast to try to save them, but the authorities insisted

44

that the brothers inform on their comrades. The father

responded, "I can bear to see my sons die, but not to live

traitors and slaves in the land of their birth."[83]

Lord Edward Fitzgerald, one of the leaders of the United

Irishmen, stated, "If I were MacKenna, I would not barter

the sterling value of his noble soul for the tinselled

honours which the highest hand of power could bestow."[84]

In May 1797 the sentence was carried out. A contemporary

account by an eye witness:

> All the troops of the Garrison
> were assembled on the morning fixed for
> the tragedy. They were marched through
> the leading streets of the town (Belfast)
> to Blaris Moor . . . As the grim proces-
> sion passed, the inhabitants without
> exception closed their shops and pulled
> down the blinds of their windows . . .
> On marched the armed ranks with glitter-
> ing bayonets, and in their midst on carts
> or tumbrils, and seated on black deal
> coffins were the bound and manacled victims.
> . . Two of the doomed men were cousins
> (brothers?), and the solitary favour that
> they asked was to be allowed to sit near
> each other, and to be placed together in
> the ranks of death.[85]

Lord Edward Fitzgerald was mortally wounded and the other

leaders were arrested before the rising even began. The

capture of Wolfe Tone with a French force of about 3,000

troops off the coast of Donegal was a disaster to the

movement. Some of the engagements of the rising are

still well known,like Vinegar Hill, Ballynahinch, Antrim,

Killala, Saintfield and Ballinamuck. Although most of

the leaders were executed, the men themselves were pardoned.

45

Juan Mackenna

The eighteenth century also witnessed the loss of
the verbal traditions of the Irish, for the English
"have completely destroyed the detailed verbal traditions
that were discussed at every fireside in the parish in the
days of our grandfathers."[86] In one way, however,
Monaghan was more fortunate than many other parts of
Ireland, for Monaghan was one of the few counties which
weren't planted successfully by the Scots and English.
It retained, therefore, a strong Gaelic character and
tradition down through the ages.[87] This tradition is
evidenced in a statement by Charles Gavan Duffy (1816-
1903) a native of Monaghan:

> "When I was a boy there were half a dozen
> of my relations among the Catholic priests
> of the diocese of Clogher, and I listened
> with complacency to their talk of the
> MacMahons, chiefs of Oriel, and the Mac-
> Kennas, chiefs of Truagh, as our near
> kinsmen . . . Even while the penury was
> sorest old social distinctions were
> cherished, and my father, as a descendant
> of 'the old stock,' was one of the few leaders
> of the people in his district.[88]

EMIGRATION, REVOLUTION, INDEPENDENCE

In 1835 John O'Donovan, the famous antiquary,
visited County Monaghan, and the letters he wrote provide
us with some very valuable information on the MacKennas.
He wrote on 1 May 1835 that, "If there was a MacKenna
(i.e. a chief) now, he could call a numerous band of his
own name to the field. They are amazingly numerous."[89]
He also discovered that several of the MacKennas he
interviewed could trace their pedigree to the last Chief
or Baron (as they called him) who lived in the time of
James II. Two of these pedigrees follow:

1. James MacKenna of Cavan-Moutray
2. Son of Shane
3. Son of Patrick
4. Son of Michael
5. Son of Dunslevy
6. Son of Michael
7. Son of Melaghlin, the second son of the last chief.

_____

James MacKenna, the eldest branch
James
Owen
Hugh
Donogh
not known

The eldest men in the barony told O'Donovan that
The MacKenna lived in a house near Glaslough. They also
told him that the MacKennas originated in Meath and
that there was a written history of the MacKennas
preserved in the territory. O'Donovan, unfortunately,
was never able to find the MacKenna history!

The numerical strength of the MacKennas continued
in the Barony of Truagh, Co. Monaghan and the neighboring
Barony of Clogher, Co. Tyrone. In 1834 a survey of Errigal
Truagh revealed 8,338 Catholics, 1,123 Protestants and
191 Presbyterians in the parish. The survey does not
reveal the names of the people, but, based on O'Donovan's
notes, one can be fairly sure that the majority were
MacKennas. In 1860 there were fifty-seven MacKenna
families living in Clogher parish, Co. Tyrone, and they
were the most numerous name in that parish.

Although the MacKennas were able to maintain their
numerical superiority, the actual population growth of
the area was severely limited by the famines of the 1840's,
which decimated the Irish countryside. "Black '47 came
with its famine and its fevers, happy homes were laid
desolate, the graveyards were filled; the emigrant ships
were crowded with the young people . . ."[90] In 1879 and
1880 there were also disastrous agricultural seasons that
ruined many families.

What the famines didn't accomplish, the policies
of repressive landlords did. Rents were continually
raised despite the poor agricultural conditions,
and most farmers couldn't pay; thus, "Writs fell over
the parish like snowflakes in a winter storm."[91] There
followed an endless succession of raises in rent, sei-
zures and evictions. Attempts of the government to
alleviate the distress were failures. The situation
in Errigal Truagh was particularly severe:

> . . . as a result of our investigation
> of the relations between landlord and tenant,
> that, with the exception of Donegal, there
> is no part of the North of Ireland which
> suffered so much, under the grinding oppres-
> sion of landlordism as did Errigal Truagh.[92]

The people reacted to the terrible state of Ireland
in predictable ways. Millions emigrated to more promis-
ing lands, "When the emigrant ship carried out of the
country the cream of the merry lads and lasses that famine
and pestilence had spared."[93] For those that remained
there were the choices of acquiescence or resistance.

The growth of secret societies was a direct result
of government oppression and the horrible economic
conditions in Ireland. The Whiteboys and Ribbonmen were
two of the many societies organized to resist eviction and
to protect tenants. They frequently used violent tactics,
as did the supporters of the government. A favorite

place to fight seemed to be at the fairs and races that were held in the area. At the Emyvale Fair in 1813 a number of Truagh men were shot, and the attackers were later acquitted. On 30 October 1818 a fight took place between a group of Truagh people and some members of the Orange Order from neighboring Co. Tyrone. This fight occurred after the Aughnacloy races, as the Truagh residents were crossing the bridge over the Blackwater. Several people were killed by a detachment of the Aughnacloy yeomanry, including Michael MacKenna and Rose MacKenna. Again the attackers were acquitted by a jury.

Incidents like the above further fostered the growth of secret societies. In 1848 another unsuccessful rising took place under the leadership of William Smith O'Brien. The failure was due, in part, to a premature outbreak, and the leaders were deported as convicts to Tasmania.

An outgrowth of this rising was the formation of the Irish Republican Brotherhood in Ireland in 1858 and the Fenian Brotherhood (Fenians) in the United States in 1859. The primary aim of the Fenians was to end British rule in Ireland and establish an Irish republic. Most of the leaders in Ireland were arrested and exiled, some were executed, and in America unsuccessful invasions of Canada were made by the Fenians in 1866 and 1870. In 1868 John MacKenna and Hugh MacKenna were accused of trying

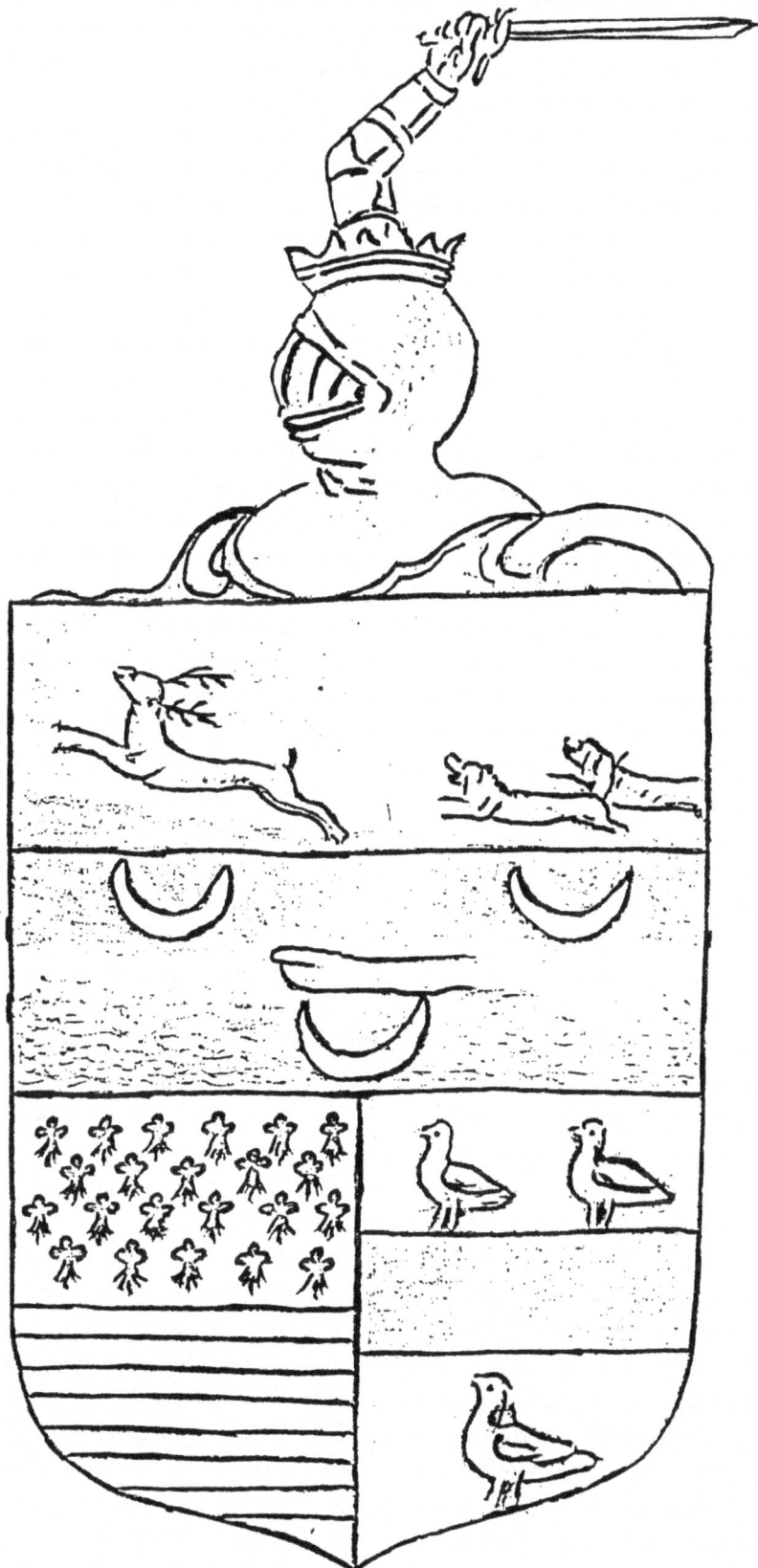

DON JUAN MacKENNA y MacKENNA

50a

to convert young men to Fenianism and Michael MacKenna
of Carrickmacross also appeared on the list of names
associated with Fenianism.[94]

Violence continued in Truagh throughout the
nineteenth century, and the recounting of a particular
incident that took place on the 12th of July around 1870
will help to illustrate this point. A blacksmith named
MacMahon had alienated the people in and around the townland of Shanco. He was shot, and a series of reprisals
followed including the murder of one Philip Treanor.
The reprisals increased, and one in particular is of
interest to us as it involves a MacKenna who shot a man
named Clarke in broad daylight in a Monaghan hotel![95]
Apparently the MacKenna had been selected to be murdered
by Clarke, but MacKenna got the upper hand! No jury
would agree to a conviction, so MacKenna went free and
eventually emigrated to America. Canon MacKenna remembered hearing a ballad describing Philip Treanor's death,
in which the old custom of covering the coffin of a
murdered man with red material was mentioned. This custom
Canon MacKenna suggested might show the desire of the
clan or family of a murdered man to make his coffin an
appeal for vengeance on his murderers![96]

The rest of the story is well known - Daniel O'Connell
and his struggle for Catholic Emancipation, the Land League,

51

Parnell, the Gaelic League, Sinn Fein and the Easter
Rising of 1916, and finally, INDEPENDENCE! The MacKennas
participated in all these aspects of Irish history, and at
the same time contributed to the history of other nations:

> Clan MacKenna in its dispersal carried
> the best of its blood into foreign
> lands up to the twentieth century!

>   Ella MacKenna Mielziner

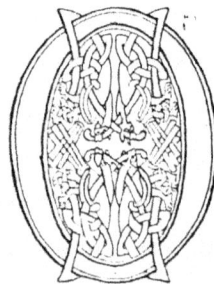

THE MAC KENNAS AND TRUAGH TODAY

It has been said of the MacKennas that they are amazingly prolific! In Matheson's report of 1890, the surname MacKenna ranked 88th among Irish surnames, with an estimated 9,000 persons bearing the name. The writer doesn't know of a more recent report which would bring the statistics up to date. In the United States in 1964, the surname MacKenna ranked 702 with an estimated 37,860 persons of the name![97]

Today MacKennas are to be found all over Ireland and Northern Ireland. Large numbers are found in Co. Kerry and in the northern counties of Derry, Armagh, Louth, Fermanagh, and Tyrone. It is natural that most of the MacKennas would be found in their homeland of Truagh, Co. Monaghan, and in the surrounding counties. In 1969 there were 73 MacKenna voters registered in nearby Co. Fermanagh. The surname is still the most common surname today in the parishes of Errigal Truagh (which includes part of Co. Monaghan and part of Co. Tyrone) and Clogher, Co. Tyrone. Remembering that the district of Portclare, Co. Tyrone, once belonged to the

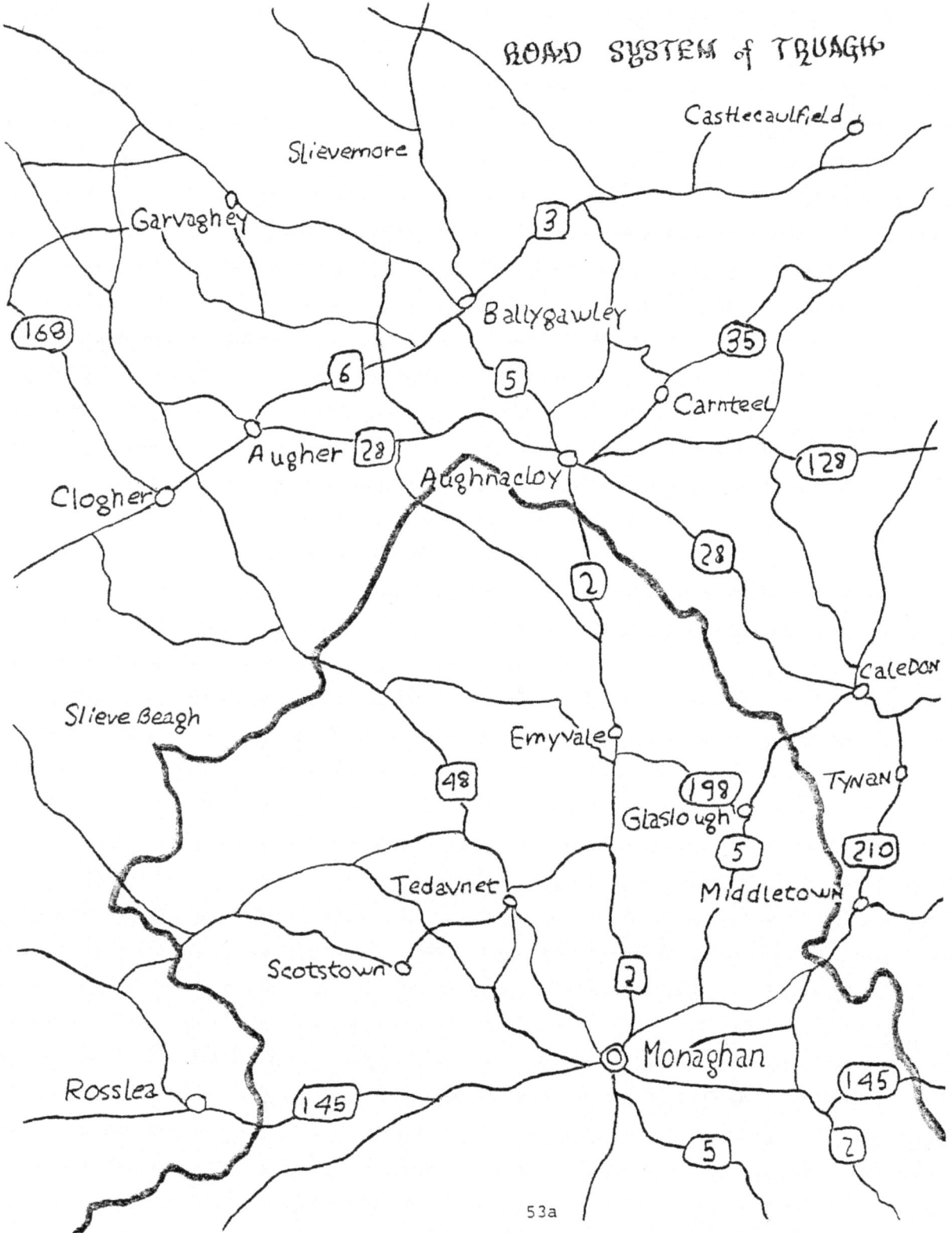

ROAD SYSTEM of TRUAGH

Castlecaulfield

Slievemore

Garvaghey

168

3

Ballygawley

6

5

35

Carnteel

Augher

28

128

Clogher

Aughnacloy

28

2

Caledon

Slieve Beagh

48

Emyvale

Tynan

198

Glaslough

210

5

Tedavnet

Middletown

Scotstown

2

Monaghan

145

Rosslea

145

5

2

53a

MacKenna chiefs partially explains this factor of numerical predominance. In the area of Clogher, Co. Tyrone, the numerical strength of the MacKennas is upheld today by the fact that nicknames are essential still to distinguish one from another.[98]

It may be that there are more MacKennas in Co. Tyrone today than anywhere else. As far back as 1825-1836 the Tithe Cards record over 300 MacKenna families living in the north of Ireland, with the majority of addresses in Co. Tyrone.

As for the Barony of Truagh, Co. Monaghan, the homeland of the MacKennas, the latest tourist literature* tells us that Truagh is a hilly district with the hills climbing to the northwest into the Slieve Beagh mountains on the Tyrone border. The highest point in the barony is the townland of Bragan (696 feet above sea level) which is also the largest townland with 2,360 acres. Bragan forms part of the wild mountain country that lies on the border between Monaghan, Fermanagh, and Tyrone. The highest points in the Slieve Beagh range are Carnmore (in the barony of Clonkelly, Co. Fermanagh), which is 1,034 feet above sea level; and Slieve Beagh proper, at the junction of counties Tyrone, Monaghan and Fermanagh, is 1,222 feet. Here a fine view of the surrounding countryside, the home of the celebrated MacKennas of Truagh,

---

*Midland Regional Tourism Organisation, Ltd.

and its beautiful loughs is available.

Alas, the famed Green Woods of Truagh are no more!
There are, however, some well-wooded areas around Glaslough and Emylough. Glaslough is located about six miles
northeast of the county town of Monaghan. The lough is
very deep and "changes colour within minutes from cobalt
to a pearly iridescence or burnished verdigris." Castle
Leslie, home of the Leslie family, is well known for its
Italian style and its trees, which are among the tallest
in Ireland. Nearby is the old cemetery of Donagh on the
Creamery Road. A MacKenna burial vault is located here,
and many headstones bear the MacKenna coat of arms. Many
of the chiefs were buried in the vault at Donagh. The
site of the Battle of Drumbanagher is just to the north-
east of the townland of Donagh.

Two miles northwest of Glaslough is the heavily
wooded area of Emyvale. Emylough has a bathing beach
and is noted for its shooting and fishing. In the townland of Mullanacross, several miles northwest of Emyvale,
are the ruins of the old parish church, the well of St.
Mellan, and the picturesque old cemetery. The visitor
might want to visit the townlands of Tully, Raflacony,
Portinaghy and Monmurry, which were seats of the MacKenna
chiefs.

The barony is dotted with beautiful loughs including

Glaslough, Emylough, Lough More, Killylough, Tullylough
and Drumcaw Lough. There are two principal rivers:
the Mountain Water, which separates the parishes of Donagh
and Errigal Truagh, and the Blackwater or Owen Truagh,
which forms the border between Truagh and the counties
of Tyrone and Armagh.

The visitor might also be interested in investigating
the many ring forts which are located in Truagh. Some of
the better preserved ones are found in the townlands of
Figullar and Raflacony. As a point of interest, there
are several townlands whose names reflect the lordship
of the MacKennas: Raflacony, which means the Fort of the
Chieftain Canagh; Liskenna, (Kenna's Fort); Derrykinnigh
Beg and Derry-Kinnigh More, (Kenna's Wood); Ardginny,
(Kenny's Hill), and Clanickny (MacKenna's meadow).

Just outside of Truagh, in the barony of Monaghan,
is the townland of Aghaninimy, home of the MacKennas of
Willville. The distance is short and the Willville
MacKennas were once so important that the visitor should
consider a trip to Aghaninimy:

> The MacKennas of Willville are still
> spoken of with feelings of kindly remembrance
> by the people of Monaghan, who recognize in
> them a family of high spirit, lively faith,   99
> undaunted courage, and generous disposition. . .

GLOSSARY

Ballagh (ballach): spotted or freckled

Bane (say bawn): white

Beg: small

Boy: yellow, from the Irish buide

Buan: steadfast, constant

Clann: children

Corragh: rough-skinned

Duff: black, from the Irish dubh

Fosterage: the ancient Gaelic custom of rearing another's
    child as one's own

Gallowglass: a mercenary soldier hired by a chief, usually
    from the Highlands or the Western Isles

Hosting: the raising of an armed force

Jacobite: a supporter of James II and of the Stuart pretenders
    to the British throne

Mac: son of, sometimes abbreviated as Mc or M' as in MacSheffrey

Mor: big

O: descendant of, as in Ó Neill

Og: young

Osiers: willow rods and twigs used for wickerwork

Plantations: the policy of extending English control by
    confiscating land and planting English or Scots settlers
    on it

Rath: a circular earthen enclosure used as a fort and,
    sometimes as the residence of a chief

Roe: red, from the Irish ruadh

Sept: a collective term describing a group of people who
   used a common surname and inhabited the same territory

Skean: a double-edged knife or dagger

Tanist: the heir apparent to a chief who was chosen during
   the chief's lifetime

Williamite: a supporter of King William III who ruled
   England jointly with his wife Mary II (1689-1702)

NOTES

[1] Paul Walsh, _Irish Chiefs and Leaders_ (Dublin: 1960), p. 232.

[2] John Marshall, _Clochar na Righ_ (Dungannon: 1930), p. 83.

[3] Very Rev. James Edward Canon MacKenna, _Diocese of Clogher; Parochial Records_. 2 vols. (Enniskillen: The Fermanagh Herald, 1920), I, p. 244.

[4] O'Dugan. _Topographical Poem_.

[5] Ibid.

[6] _Annals of the Kingdom of Ireland by the Four Masters_ (Dublin: 1851). Hereafter cited as A.F.M.

[7] Elsdon C. Smith, _New Dictionary of American Family Names_ (N.Y.: Harper, 1973), p. 329.

[8] La Reina Rule and William K. Hammond, _What's In a Name? Surnames of America_ (N.Y.: Pyramid, 1973), p. 289.

[9] Anthony Mathews, _Origin of the McKennas With a History of the Sept_ (Dublin: The Author, 1972).

[10] Denis C. Rushe, _History of Monaghan for Two Hundred Years: 1660-1860_ (Dundalk: 1921).

[11] E.P. Shirley, _History of the County of Monaghan_ (London: 1879), p. 133.

[12] MacKenna, op. cit., p. 242.

[13] _Annals of Ulster, 431-1541_ (Dublin: 1887-1901).

[14] Thomas Matthews, _The O'Neills of Ulster_ (Dublin: 1907).

[15] Samuel Lewis, _A Topographical Dictionary of Ireland_ (1873), p. 657.

[16] John O'Donovan, Ordnance Survey Letter (1 May 1835).

[17] J.Wallace Taylor, "Notes for a History of Errigal Truagh."

[18] O'Donovan, op. cit.

[19] MacKenna, op. cit., p. 227.

[20] Ibid., p. 231.

[21] Ibid., p. 241.

[22] Rev. Seosamh O'Dufaigh, "Notes on the MacKennas of Truagh," Clogher Record, (1974), p. 222.

[23] MacKenna, op. cit., p. 254.

[24] "The Register of Clogher," Clogher Record, (1971-1972), pp. 413-415.

[25] Clogher Record. Cumann Seanchais Chlochair (Clogher Historical Society). 1953- .

[26] O'Dufaigh, op. cit., p. 223.

[27] MacKenna, op. cit., p. 255.

[28] Annals of Ulster.

[29] A.F.M.

[30] Anthony Mathews, op. cit.

[31] Thomas Matthews, op. cit.

[32] A.F.M.

[33] Ibid.

[34] Ibid.

[35] Annals of Lough Ce, 1014-1590 (Dublin: 1939).

[36] A.F.M.

[37] MacKenna, op. cit., p. 257.

[38] W. Collins. (cited in MacKenna, op. cit., p. 257).

[39] J.C. Beckett, The Making of Modern Ireland; 1603-1923 (N.Y.: Knopf, 1966), p. 26.

[40] MacKenna, op. cit., p. 253.

[41] Most Rev. Dr. Patrick MacKenna, Bishop of Clogher, letter to Mrs. Ella MacKenna Mielziner, 4 Feb. 1933.

[42] MacKenna, op. cit., p. 253.

[43] Shirley, op. cit., p. 134.

[44] Survey of Monaghan, 1585.

[45] Rev. James Smyth, "Crannogs in North Monaghan," Clogher Record, (1954), p. 4.

[46] Calendar of State Papers of Ireland, p. 372. Hereafter cited as CSPI.

[47] CSPI, p. 353, 23 Jun. 1590.

[48] MacKenna, op. cit., p. 245.

[49] Beckett, op. cit., p. 18.

[50] CSPI, 4 Jul. 1592.

[51] CSPI, 10 Apr. 1593.

[52] Smyth, op. cit., p. 5.

[53] Philip Moore, "The MacMahons of Monaghan (1593-1603)," Clogher Record, (1956), p. 88-89.

[54] CSPI, 16 Oct. 1593.

[55] MacKenna, op. cit., p. 258.

[56] T.H. Mullin and J.E. Mullan. The Ulster Clans. (Belfast: 1966), pp. 171-172.

[57] Beckett, op. cit., p. 14.

[58] Ibid., p. 34.

[59] MacKenna, op. cit., p. 255.

[60] Calendar of Carew Manuscripts, cited in J. Marshall, op. cit., p. 80.

[61]Shirley, op. cit., p. 136.

[62]MacKenna, op. cit., p. 259.

[63]Gilbert, "History of Contemporary Affairs," VI, pp. 462-463. Cited in MacKenna, op. cit., p. 258-259.

[64]Gilbert, I p. 396. Cited in MacKenna, op. cit., p. 259.

[65]"The Muster Roll of Ulster," cited in MacKenna, op. cit., p. 260.

[66]Analecta Hibernica.

[67]Proclamation by the Lords Justices and Council, cited in Anthony Mathews, op. cit.

[68]Anthony Mathews, op. cit.

[69]MacKenna, op. cit., p. 258.

[70]Audley Mervyn, Clogher Record (1962).

[71]Rev. O'Mellan, Irish Diary of the Confederate Wars. Cited in Anthony Mathews, op. cit.

[72]Hearth Money Rolls, County Monaghan, 1663-1665. Cited in Anthony Mathews, op. cit.

[73]Mullin, op. cit., p. 166.

[74]Sir Shane Leslie. The End of a Chapter.

[75]MacKenna, op. cit.

[76]MacKenna, ibid., p. 261.

[77]Ibid., p. 262.

[78]Ibid.

[79]Ibid.

[80]Ibid., p. 254.

[81]Ibid., p. 260.

[82]Ibid., p. 262.

[83] Anthony Mathews, op. cit.

[84] Ibid.

[85] Marshall, op. cit., pp. 90-91.

[86] MacKenna, op. cit., p. 271.

[87] John I.D. Johnston, "Hedge Schools of Tyrone and Monaghan," Clogher Record, 1969, pp. 34-35.

[88] Sir Charles Gavan Duffy, My Life in Two Hemispheres, (London: 1898), pp. 2-3.

[89] O'Donovan, op. cit.

[90] MacKenna, op. cit., p. 222.

[91] Ibid., p. 224.

[92] Ibid.

[93] Ibid., p. 174.

[94] Fenianism: Index of Names, p. 632, 633, 634.

[95] MacKenna, op. cit., p. 242.

[96] Ibid.

[97] U.S. Department of Health, Education and Welfare, Social Security Administration, "Distribution of Surnames in the Social Security Account Number File," 1964.

[98] Johnston, op. cit., p. 41.

[99] MacKenna, op. cit., V.I, p. 109.

BIBLIOGRAPHY

Analecta Hibernica. Dublin. 1930 --.

Ancketill. *A Short History of the Family of Ancketill or Anketell*. Belfast: 1901.

The Annals of Loch Ce, 1014-1590. Ed. By W.M. Hennessy. Dublin: 1939.

Annals of the Kingdom of Ireland by The Four Masters . . . to 1616. Ed. by John O'Donovan. Dublin: 1851.

Annals of Ulster, 431-1541. Ed. by W.M. Hennessy and B. MacCarthy. Dublin: 1887-1901.

Archives Nationales, Paris. G8 236 No. 756 p. 168, G8 638 No. 756 p. 168.

Archivo Historico Nacional, Madrid. *Ordenes Militares Alcántara, Pruebas de Caballeros*. MacKenna y MacKenna, Nugent, Dowdall (Juan). 1764. Exp. 852, No. 3188, p. 2808.

Bagwell, Richard. *Ireland Under the Tudors*. 3 vols. London: Holland Press, 1885.

Beckett, J.C. *The Making of Modern Ireland*: 1603-1923. N.Y.: Knopf, 1966.

Bibliotheque Nationale, Paris. *Collection Nouveau d'Hozier*, Papers relating to MacKenna, etc. 18th c. No. 833, p. 160.

_____. Ms. 41,306 MacKenna 2116.

_____. *Pièces Originales*. Papers relating to the history and genealogy of members of the following families of Irish origin in France: MacKenna, etc. 17th - 18th c. No. 547, p. 134.

Bord Failte Eireann. *Official Guide to Cavan and Monaghan*.

Burke, J.B. *The Landed Gentry of Ireland*. London: Burke's Peerage Ltd., 1958.

Butler, W.F.T. Confiscation in Irish History. Dublin: 1918.

_____. Gleanings from Irish History. London: Longmans, 1925.

Calendar of the State Papers Relating to Ireland, 1509-1670. London: 1860-1908.

Carleton Newsletter. University of Florida, Gainesville, Florida. 1970-1975. Succeeded by Eire 19, a journal of 19th-century Irish life.

Carleton, William. The Autobiography of William Carleton. London: MacGibbon and Kee, 1968.

_____. Carleton's Stories of Irish Life. Dublin: Talbot, 1919.

Carleton, William. The Fair of Emyvale - The Master and Scholar. London: 1870.

_____. Traits and Stories of the Irish Peasantry. Dublin: 1845.

_____. The Works of William Carleton. N.Y.: Collier, 188_.

Clissold, Stephen. Bernardo O'Higgins and the Independence of Chile. N.Y.: Praeger, 1969.

The Clogher Record. Cumann Seanchais Chlochair (Clogher Historical Society). Monaghan. 1953-   .

Clogher Rural District Council. Clogher Rural District, Official Guide.

Collier, Simon. Ideas and Politics of Chilean Independence; 1808-1833. Cambridge: Cambridge University Press, 1967.

Coote, Sir Charles. Statistical Survey of the County of Monaghan. Dublin: 1801.

Crone, J.S. A Concise Dictionary of Irish Biography. 1937.

Curtis, Edmund. A History of Ireland. N.Y.: Barnes and Noble, 1936.

Dictionary of National Biography. V. 12. Oxford University
    Press. 1885-1890.

Dobs, Maighréad. "The Genealogies of the Southern Ui Néill,"
    in Zeitschrift Furceltische Philologie Halle (Salle)
    1933. Bd. 20, pp. 1-29.

Dodds, E.R. (ed.) Journal and Letters of Stephen MacKenna.
    Constable, 1936.

Duffy, Sir Charles Gavan. My Life in Two Hemispheres.
    London: T. Fisher Unwin, 1898.

Dunne, Finley Peter. Mister Dooley on Ivrything and Ivrybody.
    N.Y.: Dover, 1963.

Eggenberger, David. A Dictionary of Battles. N.Y.: Crowell,
    1967.

Ellis, Elmer. Mister Dooley's America: A Life of Finley
    Peter Dunne. Shoe String Press, 1969. Reprint of 1941
    edition.

Encyclopedia of Ireland. Dublin: Figgis, 1968.

Falley, M.D. Irish and Scotch-Irish Ancestral Research:
    A Guide to the Genealogical Records, Methods and Sources
    in Ireland. 2 Vol. Evanston, Ill.; 1961-1962.

Fee, Rev. Thomas J. The Kingdom of Airgialla and Its Sub-
    Kingdoms. University College, National University of
    Ireland, Dublin, 1950. Unpublished thesis.

Figueroa, Pedro Pablo. Diccionario Biografico de Estranjeros
    en Chile. Santiago: 1900.

Flood, W.H. Grattan. A History of Irish Music. N.Y.:
    Praeger, 1970. 1st ed. 1905.

Freeman, T.W. Ireland: A General and Regional Geography.
    London: Methuen, 1960.

Hamilton, Lord Edward. The Irish Rebellion of 1641. N.Y.:
    Dutton, 1920.

Harris, Henry. The Royal Irish Fusiliers. London: Leo
    Cooper Ltd., 1972.

Haverty, Martin. The History of Ireland; Ancient and Modern.
    N.Y.: Thomas Kelly, 1867.

Hayes, Richard J. (ed.) Manuscript Sources for the History of Irish Civilization. Boston: G.K. Hall, 1965 (11 vol).

Hayes-MacCoy, G.A. Irish Battles; A Military History of Ireland. London: Longmans, 1969.

Heraldic Artists Ltd. A Genealogical History of the Milesian Families of Ireland. Dublin: 1968.

_____. Handbook on Irish Genealogy. Dublin: 1970.

Hill, George. An Historical Account of the Plantation in Ulster. Belfast: 1877.

Johnston, J.I.D. Clogher Cathedral Graveyard. Omagh: Graham and Sons, 1972.

Journal of the American Irish Historical Society. N.Y. The American Irish Historical Society, 1898-   .

Joyce, Patrick W. Ancient Irish Music. 1872.

_____. Old Irish Folk Music and Song. N.Y.: Longmans, 1909.

_____. Origin and History of Irish Names of Places. London: Longmans, 1898-1913. 3 Vols.

Keating, Geoffrey. General History of Ireland. Dublin: James Duffy, 1865. (Translation by Dermod O'Connor).

Kiely, Benedict. Poor Scholar; A Study of William Carleton. N.Y.: Sheed and Ward, 1948.

Kinsbruner, Jay. Bernardo O'Higgins. N.Y.: Twayne, 1968.

Leslie of Balquhain. Historical Records of the Family of Leslie from 1067 to 1868-9. Edinburg: Edmonston and Douglas, 1869.

Leslie, Seymour. Of Glaslough in the Kingdom of Oriel. Glaslough: 1913.

Leslie, Shane. The End of A Chapter. N.Y.: Scribners, 1916.

_____. Songs of Oriel. Dublin: Maunsel, 1908.

Lewis, Samuel. A Topographical Dictionary of Ireland.
     2 Vols. Originally published 1873, reprinted Port
     Washington, N.Y.: Kennikat Press, 1970.

Louth Archaeological Journal. County Louth Archaeological
     Society. Dundalk, 1904-   .

Lynch, John. The Spanish-American Revolution, 1808-1826.
     N.Y.: Norton, 1973.

MacClintock, Major H.F. Old Irish and Highland Dress.
     Dundalk: Tempest, 1950.

MacCormick, Finbar. "A Group of Eighteenth Century-Clogher
     Headstones." Clogher Record, 1976, pp. 5-16.

MacDermott, Philip. Topographical and Historical Map of
     Ancient Ireland. 1846.

MacKenna, Very Rev. James Edward Canon. Canon MacKenna MSS.

_____. Diocese of Clogher; Parochial Records. 2 vols.
     Enniskillen: The Fermanagh Herald, 1920.

_____. History of the Diocese of Clogher. Unpublished.

MacKenna, John J. Fond Memories of MacGarry's Place. (no
     place, 1923).

_____. Stories by the Original "Jawn" MacKenna from
     "Archey Road" of the Sun Worshippers Club of MacKinley
     Park. Chicago: 1918.

MacKenna, Most Rev. Dr. Patrick. Letter to Mrs. Ella
     MacKenna Mielziner, 4 Feb. 1933.

MacKenna, Philip. "Historical Notes on the MacKennas."
     Corrella, Kimmage Rd., Dublin.

MacLysaght, Edward. Irish Families: Their Names, Arms
     and Origins. Dublin: Hodges Figgis, 1957.

_____. More Irish Families. Galway: 1960.

_____. Supplement to Irish Families. Dublin: 1964.

_____. The Surnames of Ireland. N.Y.: Barnes and Noble,
     1969.

MacNeill, Eoin. Celtic Ireland. Dublin: Martin Lester, 1921.

Marques, Luiz "An Irish Buddhist' Some Recollections of Stephen MacKenna." Kilkenny Magazine. No. 10 Autumn-Winter 1963. pp. 18-27.

Marshall, John J. Clochar na Righ. Dungannon; 1930.

Matheson, R.E. Special Report on Surnames in Ireland. Dublin: 1909.

Mathews, Anthony. Origin of the MacKennas With a History of the Sept. Dublin: The Author, 1972.

Matthews, Thomas. The O'Neills of Ulster. Dublin: 1907.

Mervyn, Audley. Relation in the House of Commons. (Speaker of the Irish House of Commons, 1639-1640).

Mielziner, Ella MacKenna Friend. Dan Maguinnis, 1834-1889: A Biographical Sketch with Ancestral Notes on His MacKenna Line. Provincetown, Mass.: Advocate Press, 1935.

_____. Some MacKenna Pedigrees. Los Angeles: 1944.

Moore, Philip. "The MacMahons of Monaghan," Clogher Record, 1954, 1956, 1957, 1958, 1959, 1962.

Mulhall, Michael G. The English in South America. Buenos Aires, 1878.

Mullin, T.H. and J.B. Mullan. The Ulster Clans. Belfast: 1966.

Murray, Rev. Lawrence P. "The Ancient Territories of Oirghiall, Uladh and Conaille Muirthemhne." Journal of the County Louth Archaeological Society, Vol. III, 1912-1915. pp. 52-65.

_____. "Omeath." Journal of the County Louth Archaeological Society, Vol. III, No. 3, 1914. pp. 213-214.

Murray, Thomas. The Story of the Irish in Argentina. N.Y.: P.J. Kenedy and Sons, 1919.

Naranjo, Enrique. Irish Participation in Bolivar's Campaigns. Washington, D.C.: Government Printing Office, 1927.

National Library of Ireland. MS. G. 192.

Nelson, Edna. O'Higgins and Don Bernardo. N.Y.: Dutton, 1954.

O'Callaghan, J.C. History of the Irish Brigades in the Service of France. Dublin: 1854.

O'Ceallaigh, Seamus. Gleanings from Ulster History. Cork: Mercier Press, 1851.

O'Donovan, John. Letters Containing Information Relative
     to the Antiquities of the Counties of Armagh and Monaghan.
     1835.

_____. Ordnance Survey Letter, 1 May 1835.

O'Dufaigh, Seosamh. "Notes on the MacKennas of Truagh."
     Clogher Record, 1974, pp. 221-227.

O'Dugan, John. The Topographical Poems. Ed. by John O'Donovan.
     Dublin: 1862.

O'Gallachair, P. "The MacKenna Clergy; Clogherici, A
     Dictionary of the Catholic Clergy of the Diocese of Clogher
     (1535-1835)." Clogher Record, 1976, pp. 67-75.

O'Hart, John. Irish and Anglo-Irish Landed Gentry When Cromwell
     Came to Ireland. Dublin: 1892.

_____. Irish Pedigrees. Dublin: 1892.

O'Mellan, Fr. Irish Diary of the Confederate Wars.

Otway-Ruthven, A.J. A History of Medieval Ireland. London:
     Benn, 1968.

Prendergast, J.P. The Cromwellian Settlement in Ireland.
     London: 1870.

Proceedings of the Royal Irish Academy. Irish Mss. Series.
     Vol. I., pt. 1, p. 84.

Public Record Office of Ireland. MacKenna Family Records.
     56th Reports, p. 151; 57th. Reports, pp. 232, 383.

"The Register of Clogher," Clogher Record, 1971-1972,
     pp. 413-415.

Royal Irish Academy. MS. 23D9, pp. 292-293 and 23M4, p. 214.

Rule, La Reina and Wm. K. Hammond. What's in a Name?'
     Surnames of America. N.Y.: Pyramid Books, 1973.

Rushe, Denis C. History of Monaghan for Two Hundred Years:
     1660-1860. Dundalk: 1921.

_____. Monaghan in the Eighteenth Century. Dublin:
     1916.

Sadlier, Mrs. J. The Confederate Chieftains: A Tale of the
    Irish Rebellion of 1641. N.Y.: Sadlier, 1860.

Shaw, Rose. Carleton's Country. London: Talbot Press,
    1930.

Shirley, Evelyn Philip. History of the County of Monaghan.
    London: 1879.

Simms, J. The Williamite Confiscation in Ireland: 1690-1703.
    London: 1956.

Smith, Elsdon C. American Surnames. N.Y.: Chilton, 1969.

_____. New Dictionary of American Family Names. N.Y.:
    Harper, 1973.

Smyth, Rev. James. "Crannogs in North Monaghan," Clogher
    Record, 1954. pp. 1-7

Taylor, J. Wallace. Journal of the Association for Preserva-
    tion of the Memorials of the Dead. V.I., p. 467; V. II,
    p. 184; V. III, p. 94.

_____. "Notes for a History of Errigal Truagh."

Thom's Irish Who's Who. Dublin: 1923.

Trinity College, Dublin. MSS. 1366 (H. 4. 25); 1372 (H. 4. 31)

United States Department of Health, Education and Welfare.
    Social Security Administration. "Distribution of Surnames
    in the Social Security Account Number File," Washington,
    D.C.: U.S. Government Printing Office, 1964.

Walsh, Micheline (ed.) Spanish Knights of Irish Origin. 3 Vol.
    Dublin: Irish Manuscripts Commission, 1970.

Walsh, Paul. Irish Chiefs and Leaders. Dublin: 1960.

Woulfe, Patrick. Sloinnte Gaedeal is Gall (Irish Names
    and Surnames). Dublin: 1923.

APPENDIX A

Noteworthy MacKennas

Andrew James MacKenna (1833-1872) - An Ulster journalist who founded the Northern Star and the Weekly Observer.

Benjamin Vicuña Mackenna (1831-1886) - A grandson of General Don Juan Mackenna who became a Chilean historian and politician. He wrote nearly a hundred volumes of history including a life of his grandfather, Vida del General Juan Mackenna, Santiago, Chile, 1856.

Honorable Sir Bernard Joseph Maxwell MacKenna, Kt. (Sir Brian MacKenna), (1905-   ) - Judge of the High Court of Justice (Queen's Bench Division) since 1961; Master of the Bench of the Inner Temple, 1958.

Rev. Charles MacKenna - A member of the Willville Family and a grandson of Shane MacTool MacKenna (Major John MacKenna), the last chief. He was chaplain to the Irish Brigade in the French army and present at the Battle of Fontenoy in May 1745, later pastor of Donagh.

Charles Francis MacKenna, (1861-1930) PhD. - A consulting chemist and chemical engineer, pre-eminent as an expert in materials of construction and explosives. He was a member of the Municipal Explosives Commission of N.Y.C. and of the technical committee of the American Railway Association. Dr. MacKenna helped to found and was the president of the American Institute of Chemical Engineers. His parents William and Mary (O'Meara) MacKenna came to the United States in 1842.

Rev. Charles Hyacinth MacKenna, O.P. (1835-1917) - A Roman Catholic missionary in America and compiler of many religious manuals. V.F. O'Daniel wrote a biography of the Rev. MacKenna.

Charles Morgan MacKenna (1879-1945) - A genito-urinary surgeon; Head of the department of genito-urinary surgery at St. Joseph's Hospital in Chicago, Illinois. His grandparents, Francis and Sara Jane (O'Neill) MacKenna came to the United States from Co. Tyrone in 1830.

Dr. MacKenna - A prominent member of the advanced faction of the Catholic Committee in January of 1792.

Captain Daniel MacKenna - Distinguished himself at Athy on
2 June 1642. He was offered a safe conduct by Preston,
but this was violated and he was imprisoned. Later
O'Neill arranged an exchange for him of one captain
and two lieutenants.

Major-General Daniel MacKenna - A native of Ulster, he became
Chief-of-Staff of the Irish Army on 29 January 1940.

Harold MacKenna, (1879-1946) - Brother of Stephen MacKenna
(1888-1967). A Metropolitan Police Magistrate, 1927-
1946; Commissioner under the Municipal Corporations
Acts; Chairman Berkshire Quarter Sessions, 1945-1946.

Henry Joseph MacKenna, (1885-1958) - Chief of Staff at
St. Mary's Hospital in Kansas City and President of the
MacKenna Distillery at Fairfield, Kentucky.

Hugh MacKenna - A student at the Irish College in Paris
during the Reign of Terror. When a mob attempted to
take over the college, he held them off with an old
pistol and made an eloquent and humorous speech to them.

2nd. Lieut. J. MacKenna - Served in Gregor MacGregor's South
American expedition and was wounded and taken prisoner
at Riohacha, Columbia on 11 October 1819.

James MacKenna - Servant to Oliver Plunkett while in his
prison cell in London. Canon MacKenna says he was
probably chaplain to Plunkett.

James MacKenna, (1878-1955) - Supervisor of James J. MacKenna
and Bros., manufacturers of brass fixtures in N.Y.C.,
General Manager of H.L. Judd division of the Stanley
Works, New Britain, Conn. His grandparents, William
and Mary E. (O'Meara) MacKenna came to the United
States in 1842 from Ireland.

Major James A. MacKenna, Jr. - An attorney in New York City
who served in the 69th Regiment (Rainbow Division) in
World War I. This "superb leader of men and out-and-
out American" (New York Sun) was killed in action on
28 July 1918. A Distinguished Service Cross was awarded
post-humously to Major MacKenna for "extraordinary
heroism in action near Villers-Sur-Fere, France."
"Remember MacKenna!" became the battle-cry of his men.

Brigadier James Charles MacKenna, (1879-1943) - C.B. 1936;
D.S.O. 1916; retired from the Indian Army 1936.

Very Rev. James Edward Canon MacKenna, M.R.I.A. (1868-1931)
  Author of numerous books and articles concerning the
  Diocese of Clogher and its history: Devinish, Its
  History, Antiquities and Traditions (1897), "The Friaries
  of Lisgool and Gaula" (1897), "The Parish of Dromore"
  (1916), Parishes of Clogher (1920), History of the
  Diocese of Clogher (1930, unpublished), and the MacKenna
  MSS. Canon MacKenna was born in the townland of
  Figullar, Truagh, Co. Monaghan.

John J. MacKenna - "The Poet of Archey Road." An Irish
  Politician in Chicago who was immortalized by the famous
  American humorist Finley Peter Dunne (1867-1936).
  Dunne began his humorous articles on 4 December 1892
  in the Chicago Evening Post. The chief character was
  Mister Dooley who made his appearance on 7 October 1893.
  He was to become one of America's most famous fictional
  characters. MacKenna, the only real-life character,
  played the role of the listener. He "didn't object to
  seeing his name in print . . . he gloried in the attention."* MacKenna was "honest, friendly, likable and
  possessed of considerable earthly humor."** In 1896
  MacKenna passed out of the stories and was replaced by
  Hennessy who became the great listener of the Mister
  Dooley stories. See bibliography for books written
  by John J. MacKenna.

Joseph MacKenna (1843-1926) - American jurist and Associate
  Justice of the United States Supreme Court from 1898-
  1925. He served in Congress from 1885-1892. In 1897
  he was appointed United States Attorney General by
  President McKinley.

Sir Joseph Neale MacKenna, Kt. (1819-1906) - Member of Parliament for Youghal from 1865 to 1868 and 1874 to 1885.
  He was M.P. for South Monaghan from 1885-1892.

Kenneth MacKenna (Leo Mielziner), (1899-1962) - Actor son of
  Leo Mielziner and Ella MacKenna Friend. His mother
  wrote Dan Maguinnis, 1834-1889: A Biographical
  Sketch with Ancestral Notes on His MacKenna Line
  (1935) and Some MacKenna Pedigrees (1944).

---

*Finley Peter Dunne, Mister Dooley on Ivrything and
Ivrybody. (N.Y.: Dover, 1963), p. 75.

**Ibid., p. 68.

Rev. Lambert MacKenna, (1870-1956) - Irish historian and
    editor, famous for:

    The Book of O'Hara (Leabhar I Eadhra), Dublin, 1951,
    The Book of Magauran (Leabhar Meig Shamhradhain), 1947,
    English-Irish Dictionary, Dublin, 1935.

Niall MacKenna, (d. ca. 1700) - A blind poet and harper
    who composed some of the favorite local songs in Truagh:

    The Greenwoods of Truagh (Coillte Glasa Triucha).
    Little Celia Connellan (Sigle ni Conngallain).
    A Thousand Healths to Thee Down at Truagh (Mo Mhile Slan
                                    Duitse Sios a Thriucha).
    Pretty, Gentle Damsel (Ainnir Deas Ciuin).
    I Do Not Think Myself (Ni Measamsa Fein).

Patrick MacKenna - A chaplain in Col. Hugh O'Donnell's
    regiment in Flanders, 1632-1638.

Patrick MacKenna (d. ca. 1765) - He was an active supporter
    of Wolfe Tone on the Bantry Bay expedition in 1796.
    During the Rising of 1798 he was adjutant to Napper
    Tandy. He eventually went into exile and became a
    prominent shipbuilder at Boulogne, France.

Most Rev. Dr. Patrick MacKenna (1869-1942) - Lord Bishop
    of Clogher from 1909 to 1942 and one of the founders
    of the Irish Theological Quarterly. "It was only in
    the present century that the MacKennas gave their
    first bishop to Clogher in the 'Fear' (the Man) MacKenna,
    Bishop Patrick of happy memory."*

Patrick Joseph MacKenna, (1897-1956) - Horticulturalist;
    Manager of the C.W. Post estate 1927-1928, Brookville,
    Long Island, N.Y.; N.Y. Botanical Garden; Associate
    Editor of Home and Garden Magazine. He was a native
    of Dungannon, Co. Tyrone.

Rt. Honorable Reginald MacKenna, (1863 - 1943) - British
    financier and politician who served as a Liberal M.P.
    from 1895 to 1918, First Lord of the Admiralty from
    1908-1911, Home Secretary from 1915-1916, and, finally,
    as Chancellor of the Exchequer from 1915-1916. MacKenna
    wrote Post-War Banking Policy in 1928.

_____

    *Rev. P. O'Gallachair, "The MacKenna Clergy," Clogher
Record, 1976, p. 67.

Roy Carnegie MacKenna, (1883-1958) - Manufacturer; A & T
    MacKenna Co., Pittsburg, Penn.; 1899 changed name to
    MacKenna Bros. Brass Co.; President of Vanadium-Alloys
    Steel Co., Latrobe, Penn. His grandfather Robert
    MacKenna came to the United States in 1832.

Siobhan MacKenna (Siobhan Giollamhuire Nic Cionnaith),
    (1923-   ) - Irish actress who has starred in plays,
    films and television. She is particularly well known
    for her roles in; Saint Joan, The Chalk Garden, Juno
    and the Paycock, Playboy of the Western World, Dr.
    Zhivago, and Of Human Bondage.

Stephen Joseph MacKenna, (1837-1883) - Sub-Editor of the
    London Evening News and author of numerous books
    including; Off Parade, 1872, A Child of Fortune, 1875,
    and Brave Men in Action, 1878, etc.

Stephen MacKenna, (1872-1934) - A classical scholar famous
    for his translation of The Enneads by Plotinus. He
    served as head of the Paris office of the New York
    World, and fought in the Greek army in the Greco-
    Turkish War of 1897.

Stephen MacKenna, (1888-1967) - A nephew of Reginald MacKenna,
    he was a prolific novelist, writing such works as; The
    Reluctant Lover, 1912, Tales of Intrigue and Revenge,
    1924, Reginald MacKenna: A Memoir, 1948, and Life's
    Eventime, 1954.

Theobald MacKenna, (d. 1808) - Secretary to the Catholic
    Committee in 1791 and a famed pamphleteer. He favored
    Catholic emancipation and parliamentary reform. He
    was opposed to the republican policies advocated by
    Wolfe Tone.

Thomas Patrick MacKenna (TP MacKenna), (1929-   ) -
    Actor-director who has many stage, screen and
    television appearances to his credit including: The
    Long Day's Journey Into Night, The Contractor Stephen
    D and in 1969 he directed Playboy of the Western World
    at the Nottingham Playhouse.

Virginia MacKenna (1931-   ) - Actress living in England
    who has appeared in: The Wreck of the Mary Deare,
    Born Free, Ring of Bright Water and Waterloo. She
    is the authoress of Some of My Friends Have Tails and
    co-authoress of On Playing with Lions.

Captain William MacKenna - On 12 February 1650 he was the
   first of nine Ulster officers to refuse to accept
   Clanricard as commander of the army in Ulster.
   The nine officers signed a memorial to Ormonde reques-
   ting him to send one of their own officers to take
   command until the nobles of Ulster could choose a
   general.

William Joseph MacKenna, (1881-1950) - Song writer; composed
   more than 200 popular songs as well as several operettas
   and musical comedies. Puss in Boots (operetta), The
   Road to Mandalay (musical comedy). Wrote "Let's go
   Villanova: and "The Fight Song" both for Villanova
   University.

APPENDIX B

MacKENNA HERALDRY

MacKenna heraldic design from a
gravestone in the Barony of Truagh,
County Monaghan
Coat of Arms: A hunter on horseback
Two hounds chasing a deer
Two crescents
Crest: A deer

Coat of Arms of Don Juan MacKenna y
MacKenna, Knight of Alcantara of the
Kingdom of Spain

DON JUAN Mac KENNA y Mac KENNA

Owen MacKenna
Coat of Arms: Argent a ship proper,
on a chief vert two
crescents and a hound
chasing a deer proper
Crest: A bird with outstretched wings
Motto: Fausta Venatio

Fausta Venatio

It is interesting to note the number of times that the ancient
deer chase of the MacKennas is alluded to in the coats of arms on
these two pages! In 1891, the Rev. R. S. Moffett related the
traditional tale of the MacKenna heraldic design and the story
behind it as told to him by a certain Mr. Hannyngton (*Memorials
of the Dead*, Vol. 1, p. 467. 1891.).

MacKenna

Coat of Arms: Argent a ship sable, on
a chief vert a hound
chasing a deer
Crest: An eagle proper

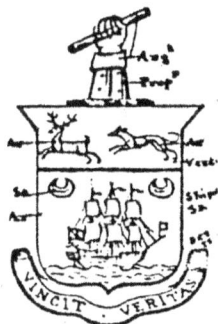

Coat of Arms: Argent a ship and two
crescents sable, on a
chief vert a hound
chasing a deer argent
Crest: A hand proper, cuff
argent, holding a baton
Motto: Vincit Veritas

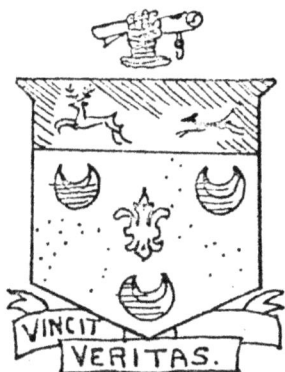

Coat of Arms: Or a fleur de lis
between three crescents
azure, on a chief vert
a stag pursued by a
greyhound argent
Crest: A hand holding a
document
Motto: Vincit Veritas

The MacKennas of Chile
Coat of Arms: Argent a fess azure
with two crescents and
a ship argent, on a
chief two oaks and two
hounds chasing a deer.
In base a crescent
azure
Crest: An eagle
Motto: Fausta Venatio

79

APPENDIX C

Name Variants

Modern	MacKenna
Gaelic	MacCionaoith
Meaning	son of Cionaoith

Variants

Ginnaw	de Machenna
Gna	Machena
Kenna	Machenna
Kennagh	Macquena	Spain
MacCinaith	Maquena
MacCionaodh	Maquiena
McKenna	
M'Kenna	Mackenna — Chile
	de MacKannagh
	de Makanna	France

Collective plural of the name

English   Gaelic

The MacKennas   Clann Cionaoith
Clann Mhic Chionaoith

APPENDIX D

The Principal Families of Monaghan

Prince: Mac Mahon

Earl: Devereux

Lords: Mac Kenna, Mac Mahon

Chieftains: Mac Ardell, Mac Cabe, Mac Donnell,
               Mac Gilmichael, Mac Oscar, O'Boylan,
               O'Connolly, O'Duffy

No Title: Hughes, Mac Gilroy, Mac Neney,
               Mac Quade, O'Cassidy, O'Hoey,
               O'Marron, O'Neny

APPENDIX E

The Grants of Queen Elizabeth in 1591

Proprietor	Townland	Parish*
Ardell MacKenna	Tireran	E-T
Art MacKenna	Killybrone	E-T
Brian MacKenna	Dernahinch	E-T
Brian Corragh MacKenna	Aghadrumcru	E-T
Bryan boy MacOver MacKenna	Kiltubbrid	E-T
Cochonaght MacJames MacKenna	Ballynahone	E-T
Cormack MacHugh Carragh MacKenna	Astrish Beg	E-T
	Killyrean, Lower	D
	Killyrean, Upper	
Donsleve MacKenna	Corgrennan	E-T
	Ralaghan	E-T
Donsleve Oge MacKenna	Aghaderry	E-T
Dunslevy MacShane MacKenna	Figullar	E-T
Eugene alias Owen MacMelaghlin Duffe MacKenna	Derrylevick	E-T
Gillegrome MacKenna	Derryhellan	E-T
Gilpatrick MacKenna	Drumbristan	E-T
Hugh MacShane MacKenna	Drumartigan	E-T
Laughlin MacDunne MacKenna	Luppan	E-T
	Rakelly	E-T
Monny MacKenna	Killylaragh	E-T
Neil MacKenna	Mullaghmore	E-T
Nele MacKenna	Clonkeen	E-T
Owen MacKenna	Dernamuck	E-T
	Drumlester	E-T
	Derrynamuck	E-T
Patrick MacKenna, Chief of His Name	Aghaliskeevan	E-T
	Mullaghselsana	E-T
	Brackagh	E-T
	Derrygassen, U.	D
	Derrygassen, L.	D

---

*E-T   Errigal-Truagh
 D   Donagh

Patrick MacKenna (cont'd)	Desert	D
	Killycooley	D
	Portinaghy	D
	Tiramoan	D
	Tully	D
	Pullis	D
Patrick MacDunslevy MacKenna	Dungillick	E-T
Patrick MacGillegrow MacKenna	Killybern	E-T
	Killymurry	E-T
Patrick MacRory MacKenna	Corraghbrack	D
Phally MacKenna	Ardginny	E-T
Phelim MacGilleduffe MacManus		
MacKenna	Mullaghcor	E-T
Rory Oge MacPatrick MacKenna of		
the Lower Troage	Killyhoman	E-T
Tirlogh MacKenna	Dernalosset	E-T
Tirlough Duff MacKenna	Drumcondra	E-T
	Lisseagh	E-T
Tool MacKenna	Davagh Etra	E-T
	Davagh Otra	E-T
	Drumarrell	E-T
	Tonynumery	E-T
Tool boy MacKenna	Mullanacask	E-T
Tool Oge MacKenna, Gent.	Derrykinard	E-T
	Corryarbeg	E-T

MacMahons receiving grants in Truagh

Brian Oge MacMahon "of the Spear Handles"
Ross bane MacBrian MacMahon
Hugh Oge MacMahon
Patrick MacArt MacMahon
John MacMahon
Brian Roe MacMahon
Ross MacManus MacMahon
Collo MacRoss MacMahon
Melaghlin MacMahon
Ross MacPatrick MacMahon
Hugh MacOwen MacMahon
Patrick MacGlasney MacMahon
Glasney MacManus MacMahon
Gilpatrick MacCon MacMahon

Other Irish receiving grants in Truagh

Owen MacQuyn
Art boy MacQuoad
Teig MacQuoad
Toole MacNeil
James Fitzpatrick Roe
Hugh MacManus
Gilpatrick Ponny MacOwen Carragh
Patrick Ponny MacShane MacPatrick

Source - Survey & Allottment 1591
and various Monaghan Inquisitions.

APPENDIX F

MacKenna Losses After the Rising of 1641

- Donagh Landed Proprietors in 1640 -

Chief
Protestant
Proprietors

Countess of Carlisle	4,200 acres of 70	tates
Robert Berckley, Protestant Dean of Clogher	6	tates
Roger Holland	2	tates
Magdalen Ackeland	6	tates
Arthur Collum	1	tate
Henry Holland	1	tate
William Pew	1/2	tate
Phelim Roe MacKenna	2-1/2	tates

Chief
Roman Catholic
Proprietors

Patrick Barnwell	2	tates
Hugh MacShane Gill MacMahon	2-1/2	tates
Garret Rooney	7	tates
Hugh MacGonnell	1/2	tate
Donslevoy MacKenna	1	tate
Hugh Bryan MacKenna and MacMahon	1	tate
which they had mortgaged to Robert Berckley		
for £100		

Prior to 1659, Mathew Ancketell had
possession of all the above except
for one tate which went to Coll Carey
of Dublin.

Source - MacKenna, V. 1, p. 269.

In the Cromwellian Settlement of 1656 there were 34 confiscations in the Barony of Truagh. The following lost their lands because they participated in the Rising of 1641 against the government:

Pattrick Barnwell
Patrick O'Carbery and his Heirs
Robert Conlan
Richard MacGill
Hugh MacGonnell
Robert Hunnelt
Ardle MacKenna
Bryan Oge MacKenna
Donnogh MacKenna and his Heirs
Donslevi Boy MacKenna
Ffully MacKenny
Gillgroome MacKenna
Hugh MacKenna
James MacKenna
Laughlin MacKenna
James Toole Oge MacKenna and his Heirs
Patrick Buan MacKenna

Patrick MacKenna
Patrick Groome MacKenna
Phellim MacEdmond MacKenna
Don Sleny MacKenna
Shane MacDonsleny Oge MacKenna
Toole MacKenna
Toole MacPhelim MacKenna and his Heirs
Torlagh MacKenna
Hugh MacShane Gill MacMahon
Bryan MacRedmond MacMahon
Aghy MacMahon
Gerrott Roony
Gerrott (2) Roony
Culne O'Shorraghan
Shane MacTrever and his Heirs
Bartholemew White
Shane MacKenna

Source - O'Hart, John. _Irish and Anglo-Irish Landed Gentry When Cromwell Came to Ireland._ Dublin: 1892.

86

APPENDIX G

MacKennas in Foreign Military Service

In the Service of France:

James MacKenna	Protonotaire Apostolique in 1755
O. MacKenna	Quartermaster in Clare's Regt. 1763-1776
_____ MacKenna	Sub-lieutenant in Berwick's Regt. 1776-1777
James MacKenna	Born 4 October 1724, Lieut. in Berwick's Regt. 5 June 1776, Chevalier of St. Louis 21 Apr. 1777, d. 1778
Francis MacKenna	Quartermaster in Dillon's Regt. 1764-1774, Captain, 1774-1780, Chevalier of St. Louis
Alexander MacKenna	Lieutenant in the 3rd Regt. of Hussars, 1814-1819.

Source - The De La Ponce MS. (Royal Irish Academy).

In the Service of Spain:

Sir John MacKenna, Knight of Alcántara - Colonel of the Regiment of Hibernia

Col. John Joseph MacKenna - Colonel of the Regiment of Ultonia

The Regiment of Ultonia was organized 1 Nov. 1709 and designated 'The Immortal.' The arms consisted of a gold harp on a blue field. The motto, Omnem Teram Exivit Sonus Eorum (Their fame has gone forth to every land) was given to the regiment by the King of Spain after the battle of Campo Santo.

There was a General MacKenna in the Spanish service in 1861, and a General Luis MacKenna in the early 20th century.

Source - MacKenna, I, p. 260.

APPENDIX H

The MacKenna Descent From
The Uí Néill or Clan Neill

1. Milesius, King of Spain. Invaded Ireland in 1028 B.C.

2. Heremon, eighth son of (1).

3. Ugane More, 20th in descent from (1), King of Ireland, B.C. 300.

4. Laogare Lorc son of (3).

5. Cobtagh Coel Breag, son of (3).

6. Eocha Feliogh, (the melancholy) IX erected the provinces into Kingdoms B.C. 14, of the line of (4).

7. Lugha Riadearg, grandson of (6).

8. Crimthan Nianair, King of Ireland A.D. 39, son of (7).

9. Fearadach, son of (8), King of Ireland A.D. 56.

10. Fiacha V, surnamed Finola, King of Ireland A.D. 73, son of (9).

11. Tuathal Teachtmar, King of Ireland A.D. 90, son of (10).

12. Feilim Reachtmar, King of Ireland, A.D. 130, son of (11).

13. Con of the 100 Battles, King of Ireland A.D. 148, son of (12).

14. Art Feliogh, (the melancholy) King of Ireland A.D. 220, son of (13).

15. Cormac Ulfada, son of (14).

16. Carbre Liffeachair, King of Ireland A.D. 264, son of (15).

17. Fiacha Straivetine, 1st King of Connaught of Race of (2), son of (16).

18. Muireadach Tireach, King of Ireland A.D. 320, son of (17).

19. Eocha Moy Veagon, King of Ireland A.D. 350, son of (18).

20. Niall of the Nine Hostages, King of Ireland A.D. 379-405, son of (19).

21. Fiacha, son of (20) founder of the Cenél Fiachach. Ancestor of the O'Molloys and MacGeogheghans of Meath.

22. Tuathal an Tuaiscirt, son of (21). Ancester of the MacKennas of Truagh.

88

APPENDIX I

The MacKenna Genealogies

Niall son of Gilpatrick
son of Toole
son of Dunlevy
son of Owen
son of Dunlevy Mor
son of Niall son of Brian Roe
son of Eamon
son of Turlough
son of Gilultan
son of Eunan
son of Niall son of Dunlevy
son of Kenna from whom Clan Kenna
son of Niallgus
son of Geoffrey
son of Fergus
son of Cruiding
son of Erc son of Fiacha
son of Niall of the Nine Hostages

The royal dynasty of Truagh
the swordsman yon MacKenna
we have heard, the scion noble
hearted and renowned, of Meath is
he, although belonging to the Oriel.

Or the same family tree as yourselves
from which is descended the noble
family of the illustrious Uí Néill.

For the sake of your excellent father
you may have from the mansion of
Brian Roe from the MacKennas of beautiful
Brionlios your full plenty of the pleasures
of the people of Ulster.

Short rations are not a fault of the
lord of the cattle levy, to be paid
henceforth without compensation to
MacMahon of the cavalry.

Royal Irish Academy MS. 23M4, p. 214.

Toole, Seathan, Ross Duff and Gilpatrick
another family of Gilpatrick:
son of Toole son of Dunlevy Og
son of Owen son of Dunlevy Mor
son of Niall son of Brian Roe
Brian and Melaghlin two sons of Melaghlin
son of Owen Og son of Niall
son of Brian Roe
Hugh son of Cuconnact
son of Seamus son of Faolan
son of Owen Og son of Dunlevy Mor
Toole and Gillegrome
two sons of Gilpatrick
son of Gillegrome
son of Owen Og son of Owen Mor
son of Dunlevy

Trinity College MSS. 1372 (H. 4. 31).

Niall son of Gilpatrick
son of Cathal son of Dunlevy
son of Owen son of Dunlevy Mor
son of Niall son of Brian Roe
son of Eamon son of Turlough
son of Gilultan
son of Eunan son of Niall
son of Dunlevy
son of Kenna from whom, the surname
son of Niallgus son of Geoffrey
son of Fergus son of Cruiding
son of Erc son of Fiacha
son of Niall of the Nine Hostages

Trinity College MSS. 1366 (H. 4. 25).

90

Toole, Sean Og, Ross
Niall, Gilpatrick
Brian and Eamon clan of Gilpatrick
son of Toole
son of Dunlevy
son of Owen
son of Dunlevy Mor
son of Niall
son of Brian Roe
son of Eamon
son of Turlough
son of Gilultan
son of Eunan
son of Niall son of Dunn
son of Gilpatrick
son of Dunlevy
son of Kenna from whom is the race
son of Niallgus
son of Geoffrey
son of Fergus
son of Cruiding
son of Erc son of Fiacha
son of Niall of the Nine Hostages

Niall of the Nine Hostages, son of Eochaidh Mugmedon,
son of Murray, son of Fiacha Sraibhtine, son of
Cairbre Liffeachar, son of Cormac, son of Art,
son of Conn of the Hundred Battles of the seed of
Eiriomhon the Milesian ancestor.

Keating's History of Ireland

Pedigree of MacKenna of Lower Truagh

Patrick MacKenna of Lower Truagh = _____ _____
    To whom the three ballybetaghs
    of Ballydavough, Ballyneny and
    Ballylattin and twelve tates
    besides were granted by Queen
    Elizabeth 10 Sep. 1591. Died
    in 1625.

_____

1. Owen MacPatrick MacKenna   = _____ _____

                                     Niall MacKenna of Portinaghy,Esq
                                     In Rebellion of 1641. To
                                     Spain in 1653.

2. Shane MacKenna of Lower Truagh
    Sold land to Tho. Blaney
    before 1626.

3. Dunlevy MacKenna   = _____ _____
    Died 10 Jan. 1608

                                     Patrick MacKenna
                                     of age 7 in 1608.

4. Toole MacKenna of Lower Truagh
    Sold land to Brett of   = Mary O'Neill daughter of Art
    Drogheda. mct before   Og O'Neill. She m. (2)
    1626.   James de la Field who died
                                     1638 and m. (3) Brian O'Neill

_____

    James MacTool MacKenna   Shane MacTool MacKenna = _____
      In Rebellion of 1641.   Last Chief, died 13 March
                                      1689 at Glaslough.

              John MacKenna = Mary _____
                 d. 1746

              _____

              1. Nugent had children John and Mary.

              2. Francis had children Mary and William.

              3. Phelim (Felix)

              4. William had children Andrew and Nugent.

              5. Mary = The O'Duffy of Clontibret

APPENDIX K

The Descendants of <u>Patrick</u> MacKenna of *Lower Trough*
d. before 1625

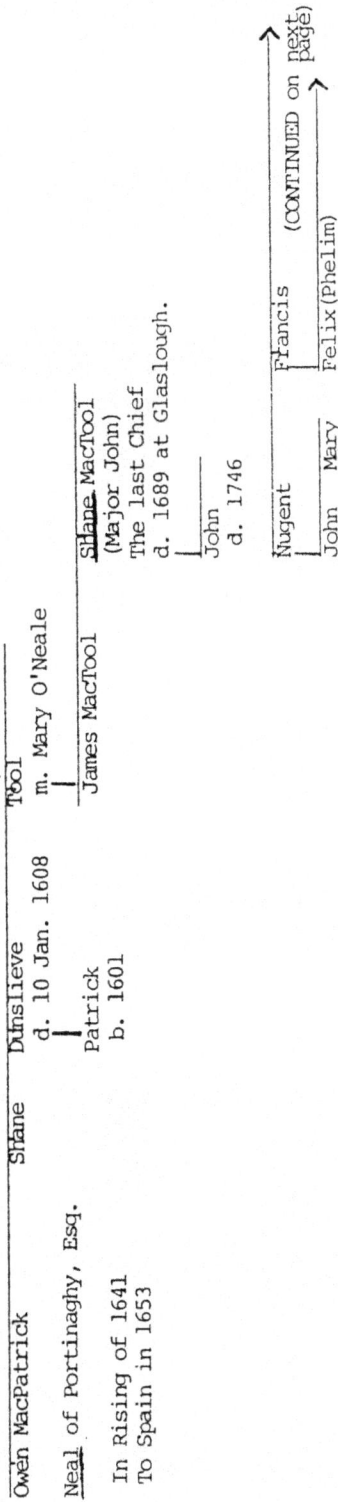

Owen MacPatrick   Shane   Dunslieve   Tool
                                     d. 10 Jan. 1608   m. Mary O'Neale
<u>Neal</u> of Portinaghy, Esq.
                                     Patrick   James MacTool
In Rising of 1641   b. 1601
To Spain in 1653

<u>Shane</u> MacTool
(Major John)
The last Chief
d. 1689 at Glaslough.

John
d. 1746

Nugent   Francis   (CONTINUED on next page)
John   Mary   Felix (Phelim)

93

THIS CHART WAS PREPARED BY
Ella Friend (MacKenna) Mielziner
Names underlined   are Chiefs of the Name

Nugent ─────── Francis
                   └─ Felix (Phelim)
John ─ Mary
   └─ John

James ──────────────── John ──────── William ──── Philip ──── William
m.   of Dundalk   of Willville   of Derry   Of Dundalk
Battersby   m. Eleanor Reilly
To Philadelphia   dau. of Philip,
U.S.A.   a near relative
Lived at Corlost,   of Count O'Reilly
Monaghan   ─────────
   │   22 children
Charles Francis Sarah   (CONTINUED on next page)

CONTINUED on next page

94

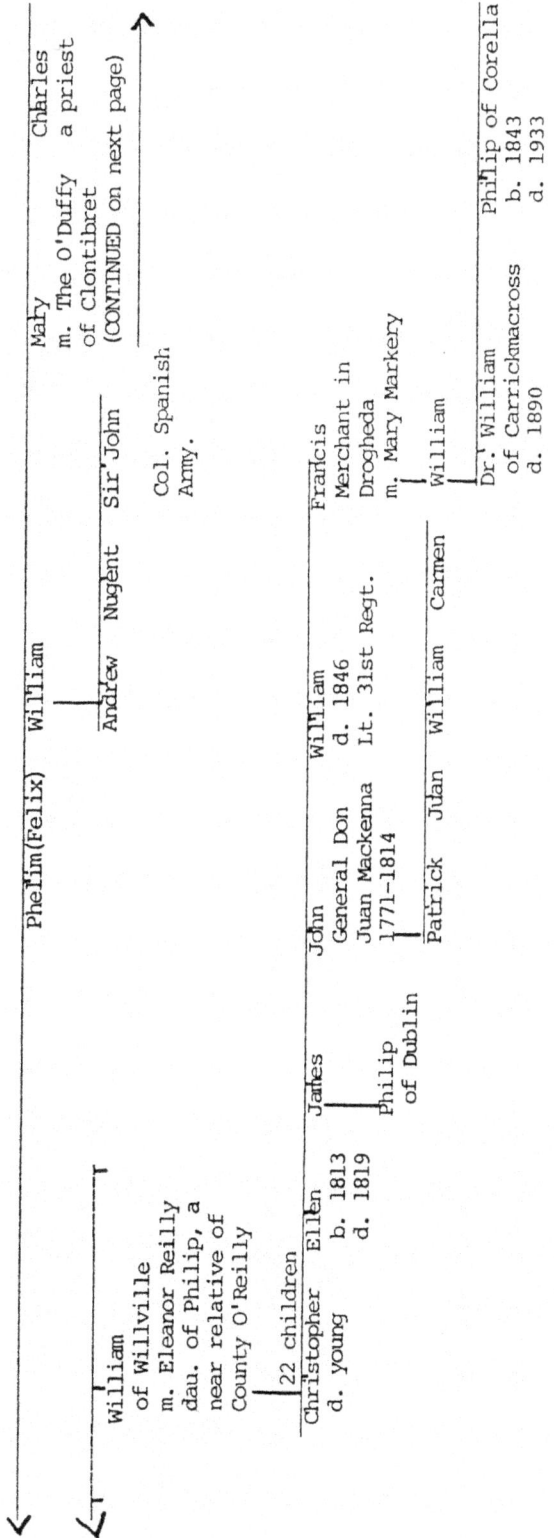

Phelim(Felix)   William

Mary
m. The O'Duffy
of Clontibret
(CONTINUED on next page)

Charles   a priest

Andrew   Nugent   Sir John

Col. Spanish
Army.

William
of Willville
m. Eleanor Reilly
dau. of Philip, a
near relative of
County O'Reilly

22 children

Christopher   Ellen   b. 1813   James
d. young   d. 1819

Philip
of Dublin

John
General Don
Juan Mackenna
1771-1814

Patrick   Juan   William   Carmen

William
d. 1846
Lt. 31st Regt.

Francis
Merchant in
Drogheda
m. Mary Markery

William

Dr. William
of Carrickmacross
d. 1890

Philip of Corella
b. 1843
d. 1933

95

Mary
m. The O'Duffy
of Clontibret

Charles
a priest

Elinor O'Duffy
m. Peter MacMahon
of Recane, Co.Monaghan

——— MacMahon
daughter and heiress
of Peter
m. Patrick McCabe
of Ballyboy, Co. Monaghan

Mary Herbert MacCabe
daughter and heiress
of Patrick
m. Thomas Fay of
Faybrook, Co. Cavan

APPENDIX L

The Descendants of Owen MacKenna of Trough

Theobald
d. 1808
|
Theobald
b. 1798 Dublin
Ass't. Under Secretary
of Ireland
|
Stephen Joseph
d. 1883
Capt. British Army
m. Elizabeth Deane
|
Theobald

Stephen
b. 1872 Dublin
d. 1934
m. Mary Bray
No issue

Translator of Plotinus

Robert
b. ca. 1874
To Australia

John

To South
Africa

Octavian

To Australia

Myles

John

Secretary to
Lord Lieutenant
of Ireland

Michael
|
Michael
d. Monaghan 1854
(CONTINUED on
next page)

97

THIS CHART WAS PREPARED BY
Ella Friend (MacKenna) Mielziner.

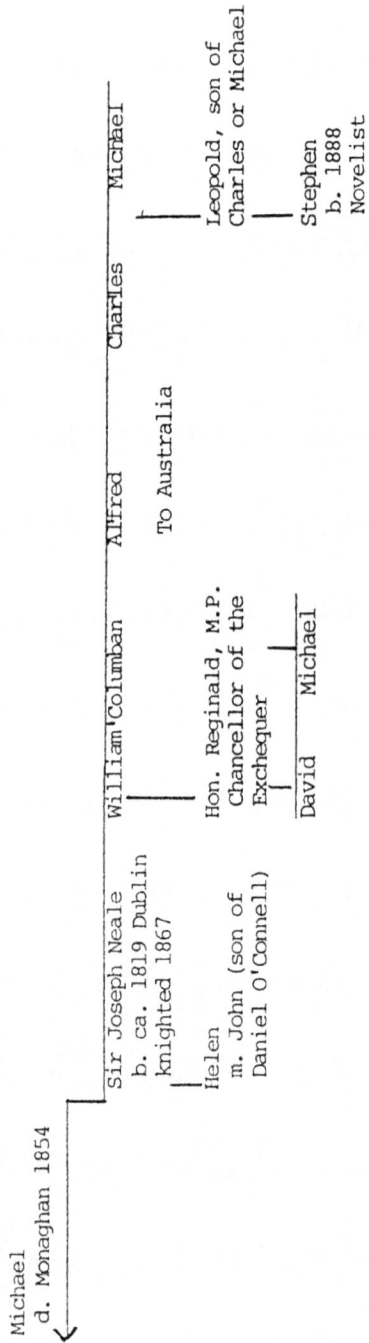

Michael
d. Monaghan 1854

Sir Joseph Neale
b. ca. 1819 Dublin
knighted 1867

Helen
m. John (son of
Daniel O'Connell)

William Columban

Hon. Reginald, M.P.
Chancellor of the
Exchequer

David   Michael

Alfred

To Australia

Charles

Michael

Leopold, son of
Charles or Michael

Stephen
b. 1888
Novelist

98

APPENDIX M

The MacKennas of Spain

Don Nelano Maquiena (MacKenna) Lord of Truagh = Doña Isabel Ustas (Eustace) of Castlemartin, Kildare

Don Juan de Adsor (Hadsor) of Guiappoe, Louth = Doña Rossa MacMahun (MacMahon) of Bolaria, Louth

Doña Cathalina Maquiena y Eustaquio* of Truagh, Monaghan = Don Patricio Hadsor y Maimon of Stackallen, Louth

Don Alverto Adsor Caballero del Orden de Calatrava   Don Diego Adsor   Don Patricio Adsor   Doña Maria Theressa Adsor   Doña Rossa Adsor

Doña Rossa Cathalina Anttonia Hadsor y Machenna baptized 20 June 1671 in Segovia = Don Ambrosio Bernal y Vallexo

Don Bartholome Bernal y Hadsor

Source – From Testament of Cathalina Maquena Madrid 1688, A.H.N. Madrid, Santiago, exp. 1034.

*Doña Cathalina Maquiena was the niece and heiress of Don Hugo O Neill, Earl of Tyrone and General of the Artillery (A.H.N. Madrid, Calatrava, exp. 23 6 July 1668 and A.H.N. Madrid, Calatrava, exp. 23 11 Jan. 1685.

99

Lineage of Don Juan MacKenna, Knight of Alcántara

Don Dunslevy, Great Baron of Trugha

Don Hugo

Don Constante

Don Julian MacKenna Squire of Trugha	=	Doña Anna MacMahon of Glaslough
Don Patricio MacKenna Squire of Trugha	=	Doña Sara O'Neill of Loughgall
Don Felemeo MacKenna of Castleshane	=	Doña Cathalina Salsbery of Salsbery

Major John MacKenna
High Sheriff of Monaghan

Don Juan MacKenna Squire of Trugha of Castle -shane	=	Doña Maria Nugent* of Portlomon, Westmeath
Don Guilliermo MacKenna of Castleshane	=	Doña Maria MacKenna** of Dundalk, Louth

Don Juan MacKenna, Knight
of Alcántara of Castleshane
bapt. 24 June 1725 at
Glaslough

*Lineage of Doña Maria Nugent

Don Edmundo Nugent of Portlomon	=	Doña Maria Fleming of Mullingar, Meath

Doña Maria Nugent

**Lineage of Doña Maria MacKenna

Don Francisco MacKenna of Garlandstown, Louth	=	Doña Margarita Plunkett of Athboy, Meath
Don Juan MacKenna of Dundalk	=	Doña Maria Dowdall*** of Kells, Meath

Doña Maria MacKenna

*** Lineage of Doña Maria Dowdall

Don Carlos Dowdall of Kells	=	Doña Juana Plunkett of Longwood, Meath

A copy of this was sent by
General Luis MacKenna of
Saragossa, Spain to Philip
MacKenna of Corella in 1908.

Source - Órdenes Militares Alcántara,
Pruebas de Caballeros.
MacKenna y MacKenna, Nugent,
Dowdall (Juan). 1764.

APPENDIX N

The Mackennas of Chile

<u>General Don Juan Mackenna</u>, (1771-1814) - The son of William MacKenna of Willville, Aghaninimy, Monaghan and Eleanor O'Reilly of Ballymorris. General Mackenna was fourth in lineal descent from Shane MacTool (Major John) MacKenna, the last inaugurated chief of the sept. Encouraged by his kinsman, Alexander O'Reilly, he entered the Royal Academy of Mathematics at Barcelona in 1784. In 1787 he was appointed a cadet in the Irish Corps of Military Engineers of the Spanish army. He served against the French in 1787-8 and again in 1794.

In October 1796 Mackenna left Spain for Peru where he served as governor of Osorno from 1797-1808. In 1810 he joined the revolutionary movement and was appointed to the junta in Chile by Jose Carrera. From 1811-1814 he served as commander-in-chief of the artillery and engineers, but a disagreement with Carrera led to his banishment for a period of three years in 1812. After serving only one year in exile, Mackenna was recalled and promoted to brigadier-general.

When Carrera was ousted by Bernardo O'Higgins, Mackenna was made second in command as chief-of-staff of the Chilean army. Mackenna was the real strategist, and he supplied O'Higgins with books and manuals and advice based on his experiences in Europe and Chile.[1] An interesting letter survives from the correspondence between Mackenna and O'Higgins, "Juan Mackenna, too, believed that the Congress would be a failure. It might, he wrote, remind him of scenes he had witnessed as a schoolboy in Ireland: 'everyone wants to talk, nobody to listen; everyone wants to command, nobody to obey.'"[2]

On 23 July 1814 Jose Carrera succeeded in regaining power. He arrested Mackenna and banished him, for the second time, to Mendoza, Argentina. Mackenna went to the capital, Buenos Aires, where, on 21 November of the same year, he was killed in a duel by Luis, brother of Jose Carrera. Luis Carrera was later executed in Mendoza. Mackenna was buried in the cloister of the convent of Santo Domingo in Buenos Aires. In 1855 an inscription was placed in his memory in the church. Mackenna is remembered in the Chilean war of independence as the Victor of Membrillar and the Saviour of Santiago.

In 1809 Mackenna married Josefa Vicuña Larrain and they had four children. Their daughter Carmen married a cousin, Pedro Felix Vicuña, and had a son, Benjamin Vicuña Mackenna. Don Benjamin Vicuña Mackenna (1831-1886) was a distinguished Chilean historian and politician. He participated in the revolt of 1851 and was forced to leave the country. He traveled in the United States and Europe until 1856, when he was permitted to return to Chile. In 1854 he visited the homeland of his ancestors in County Monaghan and devoted a chapter in one of his books to this visit. He was again banished in 1858-63, was elected to congress in 1864 and was an envoy to Peru and the United States in 1865-67. In 1875 Vicuña Mackenna was the liberal candidate for the presidency. He wrote nearly one hundred volumes of history covering the independence and the republican period, as well as a life of his grandfather, Vida del General Juan Mackenna, Santiago, 1856. He is buried in a church at the summit of El Cerro de Santa Lucia outside Santiago. A beautiful boulevard in Santiago, Avinido Vicuña Mackenna, is named in honor of him.

General Don Juan Mackenna also had three sons who were prominent in the history of Chile. Patricio was a priest in Valpariso and both Juan and Guillermo were ministers of state in the administration of President Balmaceda (1886-1891). Juan Mackenna had been Secretary of the Chilean Legation in Washington, D.C. in the 1870's. Balmaceda was advised by a group which tried to prevent him from resigning:

> Among those advisers, by far the
> ablest is Juan Mackenna, who has been
> many times Minister, and who, before the
> change in August last, was Minister of
> Foreign Affairs. Señor Mackenna is a
> born Dictator - not merely abler than
> his nominal chief, but a man of iron
> character whom nothing can intimidate.[3]

Civil war broke out in January, 1891, and on 7 August, Balmaceda was defeated and overthrown near Valpariso. The Mackennas were carried to safety in Peru by the American steamer Yorktown during the riots that followed the fall of the government.

Ties with the Mackenna homeland have been strong with the Mackennas of Chile. As recounted above, Don Benjamin Vicuña Mackenna visited Truagh in 1854. In March 1964 Señor Victor Santa Cruz, the Chilean Ambassador in London, and his wife, Señora Adriana de Santa Cruz, traveled to the MacKenna Country. Señora de Santa Cruz is a direct descendant of General Don Juan Mackenna.

They visited Willville, where the general was born, and Mr. and Mrs. Terence MacKenna of Kilrudden House, Clogher, Co. Tyrone.

I have been corresponding with Señor Pedro Undurraga of Santiago, Chile and his wife Señora Undurraga (Fanny Mackenna y Lazcano). Señora Undurraga is a direct descendant of General Don Juan Mackenna and has very generously sent me a copy of The Life of General Don Juan Mackenna by his grandson, Don Benjamin Vicuña Mackenna. Señor and Señora Undurraga have sent information on the contributions that the Mackennas have made to the nation of Chile. Here are some notable Mackennas of Chile:

Don Guillermo Mackenna Serrano - Was Treasurer General of Chile, Mayor of Santiago and Minister of Public Works in the last administration of Don Jose Manuel Balmaceda before he was deposed in the Revolution of 1891. Mackenna Serrano fled to exile in Peru, France, and later, to Spain.

Don Juan E. Mackenna Astorga - Cousin of the above, and son of Don Felix Mackenna Vicuña, he was also a minister (of Foreign Affairs and Internal Affairs) in the last administration of President Balmaceda. Before this he was Secretary to the Chilean Legation in Washington, D.C. He also had to leave the country after the 1891 Revolution.

Don Juan Mackenna Eyzaguirre - Was the son of Don Juan E. Mackenna Astorga and married Doña Carmela Undurraga Garcia Huidobro. He was a Chilean diplomat who served as Consul General of Chile in Rome and was in charge of the Chilean legation in Vienna during World War I (1914-1918). Mackenna Eyzaguirre was Minister Plenipotentiary of Chile in Costa Rica. As a writer and poet he received acclaim from the European academies.

Don Manuel Calvo Mackenna and Don Luis Calvo Mackenna - were both medical doctors and internationally known.

Don Pedro Prado Calvo - A grandson of Doña Clorinda Mackenna Serrano de Calvo, he was a talented artist, architect, painter, sculptor and poet.

Don Luis Mackenna Shell - A lawyer and son of Don Luis Mackenna Ovalle and grandson of Don Felix Mackenna Vicuña. Mackenna Shell was the Minister of Internal Affairs from 1962-1963.

1. O'Higgins: Series For Young Americans, No. 2
   Organization of American States, Washington,
   D.C., 1972, p. 9.

2. Letter from Mackenna to O'Higgins, 20 Feb. 1811
   Archivo O'Higgins I, 73. cited in Collier, p. 102.

3. The Times (London) Jan. 1891. Cited in Collier p. 108,
   109.

APPENDIX O

The MacKennas of France

Solomon MacKenna, son of John, son of
Owen, son of Patrick, son of Tully,
son of MacKenna.

Solomon's mother was Sarah Balfe, daughter
to William Balfe of Blessington, who was
the son of Patrick Balfe, Wicklow.

Sarah Balfe's mother was Mary MacDonnell,
daughter to James MacDonnell, son to
John, son to Alexander MacDonnell of
the place now called Castle Caufield.

John's mother was Elenor O Donelly,
daughter to Patrick Oge, son of James,
son of Owen Mor of Dungannon.

                       Source: Bibliotheque Nationale,
                                Paris. MacKenna, 41,306

MacKannagh, N.
MacKenna, Marie

      Receipts for pension payments and certificates
      of catholicity of N. Simiane, widow of M. de Mac
      Kannagh, 1737-52 and of Marie MacKenna, 1761.

MaKanna, Madame.

      Applications for a pension of Madame de MaKanna,
      pensionnaire du Clergé, 1761-2.

                       Source: Archives Nationales,
                                Paris. G8 638 No. 756, p.168.
                                G8 236 No. 756, p.168.

APPENDIX P

The MacKennas of Scotland

The name appears in southwestern Scotland,
particularly in Wigtownshire (15th c.), Kirkcudbright-
shire, Bute (17th c.), and Arran. The name in Gaelic
is Mac Cionaodha, son of Cionaodh. Name variants
include MacKenna, MacKinna, MacKinnie, MacKinney, MacKennay,
MacKinyie, etc. According to Scots Kith and Kin, the
MacKennas are a sept of Clan MacKenzie.

Two prominent MacKennas of the present day are
Robert Ogilvie MacKenna, M.A., A.L.A., who is University Librarian and Keeper of the Hunterian Books and MSS.
at Glasgow and whose ancestors came from South Ayrshire,
and Robert Merttins Bird Mackenna, M.A., M.D., F.R.C.P.
Dr. Mackenna is physician in charge of the Department for
Diseases of the Skin, St. Bartholomew's Hospital and
Honorable Consultant in Dermatology to the British Army.
His cousin, Miss Margaret Mackenna of Aberdeen, says that
the family descends from one Fergus MacKenna, who was
born in Ayrshire in 1660. "I think it is quite possible
that our branch of the family came from Ireland originally
. . ." She adds. Letter, August 1972.

APPENDIX Q

MacKennas in Prose, Poetry and Song

In the works of William Carleton

(1) "Sir Turlough, or the Church-Yard Bride" - This story concerns the churchyard of Errigal Truagh and a spirit which appears to persons whose families are interred there. It is the story of Sir Turlough the brave, green Truagh's pride.

> The shanachies now are assembled all.
> > Killeevy, O Killeevy!
> And the songs of praise, in Sir Turlough's hall,
> To the sorrowing harp's dark music fall,
> > By the bonnie green woods of Killeevy

> And there is trophy, banner, and plume,
> > Killeevy, O Killeevy!
> And the pomp of death, with its darkest gloom,
> O'ershadows the Irish chieftain's tomb,
> > By the bonnie green woods of Killeevy.

> The month is closed, and Green Truagh's pride,
> > Killeevy, O Killeevy.
> Is married to death - and side by side,
> He slumbers now with his church-yard bride,
> > By the bonnie green woods of Killeevy.

> > > Carleton, William. Alley Sheridan and Other Stories Dublin: P. Dixon Hardy and Sons, 1858.

(2) "The Fair of Emyvale" - appeared in the Illustrated London Magazine in 1852, and in Carleton, William. The Fair of Emyvale - The Master and Scholar. 1 vol. London: 1870.

(3) "The Fate of Frank McKenna" appears in Carleton, William. Traits and Stories of the Irish Peasantry. Dublin: 1845.

(4) "Shane Fadh's Wedding."*

(5) "The Midnight Mass."*

---

*They appear in Carleton, William. Traits and Stories of the Irish Peasantry. Boston: Francis A. Niccolls, 1911.

107

MacKenna's Dream

One eve-ning late I chanced to stray, All in the pleasant month of May, When all the land in slumber lay, The . moon on the deep. 'Twas on a bank I sat me down, The soft breeze was rust-ling round, The mur - mur of the o - cean *hush - oed* me to sleep. I dreamt I saw brave Brian Bo - ru, Who did the Dan - ish race sub-due, The might-y man his sword be drew, These words he spoke to me :—" The harp me-lo-dious - ly shall sound, When Erin's sons shall be un-bound, And they shall gath - er safe around the green laur - el tree."

2.

I thought brave Sarsfield drew up nigh,
And to my question made reply:—
"For Erin's cause I'll live and die
    As thousands did of yore.
My sword again on Aughrim's plain
Old Erin's rights shall well maintain,
Though thousands lie in battle slain,
    And hundreds in their gore."
I thought St. Ruth stood on the ground
And said, "I will your monarch*
    crown;"
Encompassed by the French around
    All ready for the field.
He raised a cross and thus did say:—
"Brave boys, we'll shew them gallant
    play;
Let no man dare to run away,
    But die ere they yield."

3.

Then Billy Byrne† he came there
From Ballymanus, I declare,
Brought Wicklow, Carlow, and Kildare
    That day at his command.
Westmeath and Cavan also join;
The County Louth men crossed the
    Boyne;
Slane, Trim, and Navan fell in line,
    And Dublin to a man.

5.

Then all at once appeared in sight
An army clad in armour bright;
Both front and rear and left and right
    March on to the fore:
The chieftains pitched their camp with
    skill,
Determined tyrants' blood to spill,
Beneath us ran a mountain rill
    As rapid as the Nore;
Along the line they raised a shout,
Crying "Quick March, right about!"
With bayonets fixed they all marched
    out
    To face the deadly foe;
The enemy were no ways shy,
With thundering cannon planted nigh;
Now thousands in death's struggle lie,
    The streams redly flow.

O'Reilly on the Hill of Skreen
He drew his sword both bright and
    keen,
And swore by all his eyes had seen
    He would avenge the fall
Of Erin's sons and daughters brave,
Who nobly filled a martyr's grave,
They died before they'd live enslaved,
    For vengeance they call!

4.

Then Father Murphy‡ he did say,
"Behold, my Lord, I'm here to-day,
With eighteen thousand pikemen gay
    From Wexford so brave.
Our country's fate it does depend
On you and on our gallant friends;
And Heaven will our cause defend,
    We'll die ere we be slaves."
Methought each band played Patrick's
    Day
To marshal all in proud array,
With caps and feathers white and gay,
    A grand and warlike show;
With drums and trumpets loud and
    shrill,
And cannons placed on ev'ry hill,
The pikemen did the valley fill
    To strike the fatal blow.

6.

The enemy they made a square
And drove our cavalry to despair,
They were nearly routed, rank and
    rear,
    But yet did not yield,
For up came Wexford—never slack—
With brave Tipperary at their back,
And Longford next, who in a crack
    Straight swept them off the field.
They gave three cheers for liberty,
As the enemy all routed flee;
Methought I looked but could not see
    One foeman on the plain.
Then I awoke—'twas break of day:
No wounded on the ground there lay,
No warriors there, no fierce affray:—
    So ended my dream.

Donal O'Sullivan, who has this information from the late Dominick
Kane, a native of Donegal, tells me that towards the end of the last century, at Buncrana, a street-singer would often be brought before the R.M.
who asked: «What is the charge in this case?» The answer would usually
be: «Singing McKenna's Dream, Sir.»
    There is in Cambridge University Library an Irish broadside ballad on
the death of Father Tom Maguire (1855) by a William McKenna. Another
broadside in the McCall collection, N.L.I., is entitled «McKenna's Lament
for John Mitchel».

Slow and with expression.

The following is the last verse :—

In coffins they were hurried,
From Blaris Moor were carried,
And hastily were buried,
    While thousands sank with grief;
Crying "Grania,† we much wonder
You rise not from your slumber,
With voice as loud as thunder,
    To grant us some relief!"

From the collection of Patrick W. Joyce

The Green Woods of Truagh

(Coillte Glasa an Triucha)

MS. 33, book 3, p. 6.   A Double bar here in MS.   B Crotchet in MS.

I. A chúl álainn, tais, na bhfáinní geas,
   Is breagh 's is deas do shúile!
Is go bhfuil mo chroidhe 'stigh gá shlad mar shníomhthaidhe gad
   Le bliádhain mhór fhada a' súil leat.
Dá bhfuighinn-se ó cheart cead síneadh leat
   Is éadtrom breagh gasta shiubhalfainn:
Is é mo mhíle chreach gan mé is tú, a shearc,
   Faoi choillte breagh glasa'n Triúcha,

II. A Dhia gan mise 's mo ghrádh bhfuil a brollach mín, bán,
    Is gan neach i gCríoch Fáil 'n-a ndúsgadh,
  Fir agus mná 'n-a gcodladh go sáimh
    Ach mise 'gus mo ghrádh a' súgradh!
  A ghéig chailce an áigh, is deise do na mnáibh,
    A réalt eólais a thóigear dhúmh-sa,
  Ní chreidiom-sa go bráth ó shagart nó ó bhráthair
    Go bhfuil peacadh ins a' pháirt do dhúbladh!

III. A rún agus a shearc, is a chroidhe mín geal,
    Ná fág thusa seal a' dún so,
  Is go n-éalochainn leat ins a' tír úd amach
    Mar bhfuighmis-ne cró agus ubhla :
  Mar bhfuighmist an breac 's a' londubh ar a nead,
    Agus fiadh faoi an charraic a' búirfidhe,
  Luachar cráite faoi ár gcosa san áit a bhfuighe tusa
    An ní nachar chleacht do mhúdar.

IV. A rún agus a shearc, gluaiseamuinn gan stad
    Go coillte breagh glasa'n Triúcha,
  Mar bhfuigheamuinn go deimhin ól agus imirt,
    Agus cáil d'ár mbeatha dhuthchais :
  Caora cuilinn, cruasach biolair,
    Cnó agus ubhla cumhra ann,
  Is go leór leór don duilleabhar fúinn is tharrainn
    Agus fásach go mullaigh glún ann.

V. A rún agus a shearc, fan réidh agus bí 'teach!
    Is tréigeamuinn ár bailte duthchais,
  Tar anoir 'un a bhfuil na gaorthaí aige na loin,
    Is na h-ubhlaí a' teacht 'n-a cúplaí :
  An féar is glaise, an t-éan is binne,
    Is an chuach ar mbarra géag ann,
  Is go deó deó ní thiocfaidh an bás dár ghoire
    I lár na coillte cumhra!

Translation

I. Lovely gentle head of the ringletted curls,
Fine and beautiful are your eyes!
My heart is being ravaged and twisted like a withe
For a great long year hoping for you.
If I might lawfully lie down beside you,
Light, handsome and bold would be my gait:
Woe is me a thousand times that you and I, beloved,
Are not in the lovely green woods of Truagh.

II. O God! that I and my love of the gentle, white breast are not
     together,
With no one in Ireland waking.
Men and women soundly asleep,
But I and my love playing!
White, glorious branch, most beautiful of women,
Guiding star set on high for me,
Never believe from priest or friar
That it is a sin to give love for love.

III. Sweetheart, beloved and gentle, bright heart,
Do not leave this town for a while,
And I will elope with you to yonder country,
Where we shall get nuts and apples:
Where we shall find the trout, and the blackbird on its nest,
And the stag belling under the rock,
Crushed rushes under our feet in the spot where you will get
Something your mother was not used to.

IV. Sweetheart, beloved, let us go without tarrying
To the lovely green woods of Truagh,
Where we shall certainly get drink and play,
And plenty of our country food:
Holly berries, a bunch of cress,
Nuts and fragrant apples,
Abundance of foliage under and over us,
And grass to the height of our knees.

V. Sweetheart, beloved, be quiet and come,
And let us leave our native lands,
Come westward where the blackbirds hold sway in the wooded
    glens,
And the apples grow in pairs:
The greenest grass, the most tuneful bird,
And the cuckoo on the tops of the branches,
And never, never shall death come nigh us
In the depths of the fragrant woods

Source – Edward Bunting. A General
Collection of the Ancient Music of Ireland. 1796.

The Green Woods of Truagh

Another Version

In the green woods of Truagh we
met with - out fear, Your kiss on my
lips, and your voice in my ear, Your
ten - der - arms a - bout me, and your eyes glad and

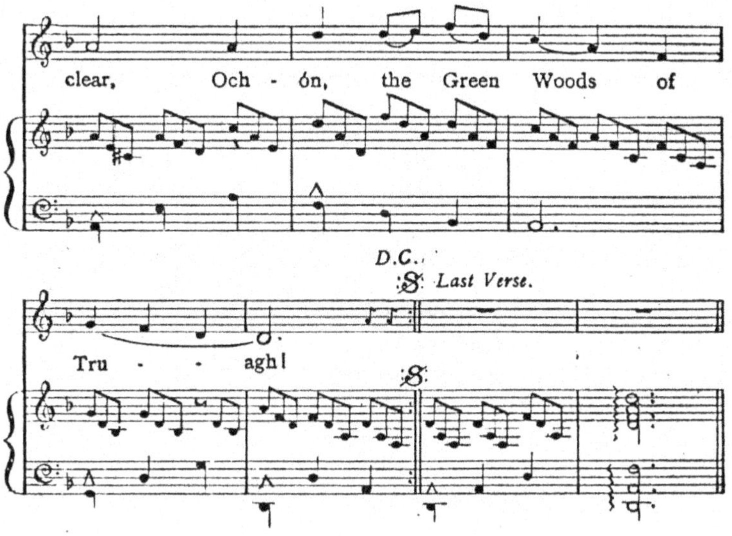
clear, Och - ón, the Green Woods of
D.C.
Last Verse.
Tru - - agh!

THE GREEN WOODS OF TRUAGH.

In the green woods of Truagh we met without fear,
Your kiss on my lips, and your voice in my ear,
Your tender arms about me, and your eyes glad and clear—
    Ochón, the Green Woods of Truagh!

In the green woods of Truagh the days go on wings,
On every brown branch a gladsome bird sings,
And the fragrant amber blossom of the honey-suckle swings—
    Ochón, the Green Woods of Truagh!

In the green woods of Truagh the bracken stands high,
And wells of spring-water in deep hollows lie,
And the red deer is browsing in the cool shadows nigh—
    Ochón, the Green Woods of Truagh!

In the green woods of Truagh no sorrow dared stay,
The lark called me early at dawn o' the day,
And o'er my sleep at night pleasant dreams used to play—
    Ochón, the Green Woods of Truagh!

In the green woods of Truagh you wait till I come—
I left home and you for the stranger's far home,
To bring a hoard of yellow gold across the grey foam—
    Ochón, the Green Woods of Truagh!

In the green woods of Truagh—if God hears my prayer—
I shall reach you, O true love, my empty hands there,
For little of the yellow gold has fallen to my share—
    Ochón, the Green Woods of Truagh!

In the green woods of Truagh—your heart on my own,
And your bright hair in ringlets across my cheek blown,
Now where in all the wide, wide world, could greater bliss
    be known?
    Ochón, the Green Woods of Truagh!

                ETHNA CARBERY.

The Praise of Truagh

(Molad an Triucha)

He that ne'er has been in *Truacha*,
   Its sweet and *beauteous* scenes to TRY,
Can ne'er conceive all the pleasing *views*,
   That the mind *amuse* and delight the EYE.

There rising groves upon sloping *hills*,
   And trickling *rills* in the vales APPEAR ;
And sylvan music, in warbling *trills*,
   With sweet rapture *fills* the enchanted EAR.

What need I mention its limpid *fountains*—
   The distant *mountains* in prospect RISE;
Its lovely villas in taste *abounding*—
   Sure no air is *sounder* beneath the SKIES.

In fine no object is seen in *nature*,
   That gives a *taste* of primeval JOYS,
But here, with pleasing soft *sensation*,
   And sweet *amusement*. the soul ENJOYS.

Source - The Bunting Collection
of Irish Folk Music & Songs.

Truagh (An Triucha)*

Gluais, a Mhai-lí, a - gus tar dom' fhéa-chain, A - gus
triall-a-muid ar - aon chun a' Iriú - chá síos, Mar
bhfuigh-mid samh-aid a - gus cao - ra caor-thuin A - gus
cnó buidhe mao-la ar bharr - - ibh craobh.

I. Gluais, a Mhailí, agus tar dom' fhéachain,
   Agus triallfamuid araon chun a' Triúcha síos,
   Mar a bhfuighmid samhaidh agus caora caorthuin
   Agus cnó buidhe maola ar bharraibh craobh.

II. Leaba ghlas don duilleabhar aighneáin,
    A' lon 'sa' smaolach ar gach uile thaobh,
    Mo lámh i n-a fochras is mé dá bréagnadh,
    Is a' súgradh léithe, mo Bhailintín.

III. An eilid mhaol 'gus na gamhna 'súgradh,
     Is an gearfhiadh lúthmhar a' dul fón ngleann,
     Na bradáin tárr-gheal loinneach 'n-a gcúplaibh—
     O! samhail an Triúcha ní fheiciom[1] ann.

IV. Is binn guth eala ann 's is binn guth traon' ann,
    'S is binn guth cuach ar bharraibh crann,
    Is binn guth cailín ann 's is binn guth buachaill,
    'S is binn guth gach aon neach d'oileamhnar ann.

* Also called Old Truagh (A Sean Triucha) and The Old Truagh
(An Seann Triucha)

Translation of Truagh

1. Come, Molly, come to see me,
   And we will both go up to Truagh,
   Where we shall find sorrell and rowan berries
   And smooth yellow nuts hanging on branches.

II. A green bed of ivy leaves,
    The blackbird and thrush on every hand;
    My hand would be in her bosom and I would court her
    And make merry with her, my Valentine!

III. The hornless doe, the calves playing,
     The swift hare running along the vale,
     The gleaming, white-bellied salmon in couples—
     Oh, I can see no country like Truagh.

IV. There the swan's voice is sweet, and the corncrake's,
    And the cuckoo's from the tree-tops,
    And the voice of girl and the voice of boy,
    And the voice of all who are reared there.

Source - Edward Bunting. A General
Collection of the Ancient Music of Ireland. 1809.

MacKenna's Farewell

Farewell, farewell ye woods of Truagh
Fast fading from my sight,
Whilst here I stand I bid to you
a sorrowful good-night;
For tho tomorrow's sun shall rise
To brighten hill and plane,
I'll be far from all I prize
Upon the stormy main.

No wonder that my eyes are dim
as my last look I take,
Or that my anguish-laden heart
With grief is fit to break;
for 'twas among those ancient woods
I spent my happiest hours-
A wayward child, a roving boy
In pleasure's fairy bowers.

Tonight I leave them all behind,
They'll bloom no more for me;
I must go and seek a second home
Beyond the dark blue sea.
'Tis fate, stern fate that bids me go
From hearts I love so dear;
Then let me pause, while yet there's time
To shed a parting tear.

Each well remembered nook and glen
Invites me still to stay-
And nature's cry from scenes so grand-
How can you go away?
Yes, yes, 'tis true, but still I must
Leave all those scenes behind,-
Our good ship's waiting in the port,
Her white sails in the wind.

I see the murmuring little stream
Upon those grassy banks-
I oft times spent the life-long day
Engaged in childish pranks,
Or tried to lure the speckled trout
From out its hiding place.
Oh ne'ar can time, from memory's page
Those happy days efface.

I see the old and time-worn oak
With gnarléd branches wide,
Beneath whose shade I used to sit
At beautous eventide.
With open book before me there,
An eye fixed on the page,
A resting with some hero would
My youthful mind engage.

What boasts it now to paint those scenes
Before my tear-dimmed eyes?
They only make my heart more sad.
As memory that flies,
They only make me feel more keen
The parting hour that's nigh;
They only darken more and more
My life's overshadowed sky.

Ah, that it is with earthly joys
And earthly pleasures too
The sunbeams bright they move away
Before our mortal view.
We haven't here a resting place,
Our home's beyond the sky.
Then why for transient earthly things
Should we lament or sigh?

Ye waving woods of Truagh,
Once more I say adieu-
When far away in other lands,
My thoughts will turn to you.
And when my barque has run its course
upon life's stormy sea,
Of early days and Truagh's green woods
My latest thoughts would be.

Courtesy of Mrs. Mary MacKenna of
            Kilrudden House, Clogher,
            Co. Tyrone.

Written by one of the MacKennas of Anketell
Grove on the eve of his departure to South
America.

APPENDIX S

The Lament for Ross MacKenna

A thousand seven hundred and three twenties
Of the age of the Son of God, less two years
since the model of the Gael who was in Christ's livery went

Into the earth, a hundred alases.
The wisdom of Solomon was in the key to his mind
The generosity of Eochaidh that nourished learning
Hector and Paris of Troy, Ganymede,
Achilles, Hercules who used to uphold the mountains.

Oh! Sparkling cinders with one flame which gives true
  delight and interest to your people,
And there is the defeat of four in every crozier blow from
  base to top
Your thin breasts, your snow white throat, your body,
  crippled by Gael and foreigner
And he is no less to you even the worn-out blind
  man being in difficult pain going to die for your sake.

Brian MacKenna wrote this in Pullis near Glaslough
  in the year 1810. These verses are about the death
  of Ross MacKenna, parish priest of Errigal Truagh
  who died in 1758.

Royal Irish Academy MSS. 23 M 39

122

APPENDIX T

The Will of Toole MacKenna

Below is the text of the will, probated in January, 1698/9, transcribed by Philip MacKenna, and found among the Canon MacKenna MSS. This is the first copy of the complete will of a Penal Day priest to be published in this dictionary:

I, the undersigned, being in good sense and perfect memory the tyme of these presents, do make my last Will as follows: Inprimis--I bequeath my soul to God, my Master and Redeemer; my body to be buried in the church or churchyard of Ergill.

2ndly: I leave as legacies to be disposed for my soul, vis., to the C.Mc. twenty shillings; to Fa James Mackenna twenty shillings, to Fa Brian oge MacMahon tenn shillings, to Fa Patt O'Conolly tenn shillings, to Fa Bernard ? MacKenna five shillings, to Fa James MacTrenor five shillings, to Fa Philip Duffy five shillings, to Fa James Duffy five shillings, to Fa Philip Biggan ten shillings, to Fa Bryan Martin-- Edmond MacGirr, five shillings.

I leave to be disposed at my burial or funeral, thirteen pounds for which sum of money I leave two mares, two foals and a horse, and if there will remain any over and above the said thirteen pounds, I allow a tomb to be erected to my body . . . expenditure . . . it can be properly done.

4th I leave three in-calf cows and grey garron to Patrick MacKenna and to my nephew, Bryan MacKenna, three in-calf cows and my lease as follows of Dirilea and Killolagh, equally to be divided between the said Patrick and Bryan-- Lr Killefarahy, Corragh and Loghteen, equally to be divided as aforesaid, and my interest in Cluinkeene as long as my landlord, James Moore, Esqr., will be pleased to be divided as aforesaid.

I leave to my dear Kate MacKenna, in considera- tion of her kind services to me, one in-calf cow, one heiffer--and I leave to my sister, Eliza MacKenna, one, and to my neice, Rose Ny Kenna, one dry cow. I leave to Cily Ny Kenna one heiffer, and one calf to my neice, Kate Mahon.

                    I appoint my nephew, Neill O'Quin, Administrator,
              and my cousan, Edmond MacArt Moder, assistant,
                         as witness my hand this 1st Oct., 1698,
                                          Toole MacKenna.

              Witness   James MacKenna
                         Patrick Keaner
                         Neil MacKena.

     Evidently after Fr. Toole's funeral there was some
money remaining "over and above the said thirteen pounds"
that he left for his burial, so that a fine tomb was
provided as he requested. It can still be seen in the
old graveyard of Errigal Truagh and contains the following
inscription, with his age omitted:

     Pr. Tullius Kenna jacet in hoc tumulo, qui obiit
     3 Decembris, Anno 1698. (Fr. Toole MacKenna lies
     in this grave, who died 3 December, in the year
     1698).

                              Source: Clogher Record*
                                        (1976) pp. 71-72.

*Clogher Record hereafter cited as CR.

                              124

APPENDIX U

MacKenna Cemetery Inscriptions
Donagh Cemetery
Parish of Donagh, Co. Monaghan

ROW A - 4. Erected by Felix MacKenna in memory of his father,
Neal MacKenna Minmurry, who departed this life 14 Jan
1817, aged 71 years. Also his wife, Mary MacKenna,
who died 8 January 1810, aged 58 years.

5. This stone was erected by Neal MacKenna of Tileydon
for the use of his family.

ROW C - 4. Pray for the soul of Patrick MacKenna Anagap who
died 30 March 1927. Margaret MacKenna, 20 April 1928.
John MacKenna, 18 August 1938.

5. This stone is erected by Charles MacKenna of Mullaghboy
in memory of his son who departed this life 26 June 1792,
aged 32 years.

ROW G - 14. Here lyeth the body of Philemy MacKenna deceased
the 15 April 1666. (This is the grave of Bully MacKenna,
a famous character is local folklore.)

ROW H - 3. Here lyeth Neale MacKenna who departed __ of October
174__.

ROW I - 18. Here lyeth the body of Charles MacKenna of Clonickny
who died December 1786, aged 71 years.

ROW J - 2. Here lyeth the body of Edward MacCana who departed
this life August 18, 1769, aged 63 years. Likewise the
body of Andrew MacKenna so to James MacKenna of Mulam__hy
who departed this life June 19 1779, aged 13 years.

6. Patrick MacKenna of Dog__y erected this stone to his
father, Terence MacKenna, who died Sept. ye 1st ____.

8. Here lyeth the body of Patrick MacKenna deceased
January ye 26th 1682, aged 84 years. Also his son,
Patrick MacKenna, who died the 27th ____ 1725, aged
____ years.

9. Here lyeth the body of Felix MacKenna of Knockafuble
who died May 1, 1785, aged 92 years.

125

ROW K - 4.   This stone _____ MacKenna _____ 2nd September.

6.   Erected by Madame Colson to the memory of our dear father, Owen MacKenna Ballinaman, died 26 June 1889, aged 85 years. May his soul rest in peace. Also to our dear mother, died 14 August 1892.

ROW L - 3.   Here lyeth the body of John MacKenna who departed this life September 11, 1767, aged 60 years.

6.   This stone was erected by Francis MacKenna of Aughaboy in memory of his father, Culla MacKenna, who died March 2, 1768, aged 54 years, and of his two sons, Culla & Patrick.

9.   Here lyeth ye body of James MacKenna who died July ye 7, 1719, aged 54 years.

CR 1957 Article by
Rev. B. McCarney.

The monuments are arranged in rows, listed here alphabetically, reading from North to South and commencing at the wall facing St. Mary's Church, Glennan.

126

Mullanacross Cemetery
Parish of Errigal Truagh, Co. Monaghan

This stone was erected- by James MacKenna- in memory of
his- mother, Anne Sweeney of Tomyamogagh- who departed
this life Decr the 18th, 1803, aged 21 years- Also here
lieth the body of James MacKenna- who departed this life
August 22, 1817, aged 55 years.

I.H.S.- This stone was erected- by Owen MacKenna of
Cullamor in memory of- his wife Mary MacKenna, who
departed this life- July 4th, 1854, aged 70 years.

Here lieth the body of James MacKenna of Mullanisky, who
died August 28th 1800. Also his daughter Anne MacKenna,
aged 6 months.

Here lieth the body of Tully MacKenna, of Kilfahavan, who
departed this life the 12th April, 1816. Aged 66 years.

Sacred to the memory of John MacKenna, late of Cavancope-
who departed this life on the 2nd day of June, 1828.- Aged
70 years.

In memory of Tetrthag MacKenna- of Greagh, wife of Tool
MacKenna- who died the first of August- 1800, aged 84 years-
Also in memory of his- father and mother- May they . . .

Here lieth the body of Hugh MacKenna, who departed this
life May the 7, 1723, aged 63 years.

Pr. Tullius Kena jacet in hoc tumulo, qui obijt. 3 Decembris
Anno 1698. (Fr. Toole MacKenna lies in this grave, who
died 3 December, in the year 1698.)

Hic quoque tumulatae sunt reliquiae Rev. Tullii MacKenna,
nuper, pastoris de Errigal, qui obiit 27 die Octobris, 1764,
aetatis 56. (Here also are buried the remains of Rev. Toole
MacKenna, late Pastor of Errigal, who died 27th day of
October, 1764, aged 56.)

MacKenna, Parishes of Clogher,
Vol. I., Most of these stones bear
the MacKenna coat of arms.

Clogher Cathedral Graveyard
Clogher, Co. Tyrone

#241 Patrick MacKenna of Nurchasy
      b. 1641
      d. 17 March 1711

#245 Philemy MacCanna of Altnakerney
      b. 1700
      d. 17 June 1770

      Constantine MacKenna
      b. 1724
      d. 10 April 1784

      Mary MacKenna (daughter of Neal of Altnacarney)
      b. 1765
      d. 18 February 1794

#315 Arthur MacKenna
      b. 1710
      d. 15 April 1733

#417 Francis MacKenna of Ballyoullen
      b. 1740
      d. 23 May 1796

      Owen MacKenna (his brother)
      b. 1730
      d. 1 August 1803

#423 Catherine MacKenna of Tullnavert
      b. 1769
      d. 16 April 1787

#500 Patrick MacKenna
      b. 1754
      d. 29 February 1814

Johnston, J.I.D.
Clogher Cathedral Graveyard.
Omagh, Graham & Sons, 1972.

All in central area of the
cemetery between the two
main pathways.

Drumsnat Graveyard
Parish of Drumsnat, Co. Monaghan

#47   Here lyeth the/ body of Tole/ MacKenna who/
departed this life May 7th 1751/ Aged 76 years/
Erected   by his/ son Own MacKenna

Mrs. Annie MacKenna of Cooldarragh had the
right of burial in Drumsnat Graveyard in 1954.

> CR 1966. Article by Bearnárd
> Ó Dubhthaigh

Killanny Old Cemetery
Barony of Farney, Co. Monaghan

#9   Erected by direction of Patrick MacKenna of
Coolreagh and Drumeever who died 14th Jany 1900.
In memory of his father and mother, Patrick and
Mary MacKenna. His brothers, Edward, William,
Denis, Matthew and John. Also in memory of his
wife, Catherine, who died 8th April 1905. R.I.P.

> CR 1966. Article by
> Rev. P. O. Mearain

Tydavnet Old Cemetery
Parish of Tydavnet, Co. Monaghan

#2   To Terence MacKenna of Knockballyroney, d. December
1788, aged 44.

#11   By John MacKenna of Knoknalon for him and his family
1827.

#39   To Peter MacKenna, d. 27 June 1771, aged 76.

#44   By John MacKenna to his father, William, d. 20 May
1758, aged 72. Also Ann Moan, d. 25 October 1787,
aged 28.

#64   By Ross MacKenna of Greaugh for himself and family,
1818.

#84   By Hugh MacKenna of Mullahinchago for himself
        and his family, 18 April 1831.

#87   By Loughlin Mackenna to his son, James, d. 17
        February 1786.

#94   To Francis MacKenna of Toneylone, d. 8 February
        1900, aged 76. Also his wife, Mary, d. 8 February
        1901, aged 59; their son, Owen, d. in Glasgow
        1 August 1909, aged 47.

#99   To Terence MacKenna of Knockbelirony, d. 7 December
        1788, aged 44 (see #2)

#103   By Bryan MacKenna of Knockbloroney to his daughter,
        Ann, d. 1 October 1790, aged 3.

#137   To James MacKenna of Mullockan, d. 17 March 1731,
        aged 60.

                    CR 1954, Article by
                      Very Rev. B. O'Daly

        This stone was erected by Terence MacKenna in
        memory of Toale MacKenna of Shig who departed
        this life February 16, 1790. Aged 61 years.

                    CR 1979

                Old Kilskeery Graveyard
                    Co. Tyrone

Row H
#72.   H./1./T./B./O./ (pat)rick MacKenna/ (wh)o dyed
        Agust/ the 3/ 1721/ Aged 50/. His wife Rose
        O D/onnelly died Febr./ The 3, 1712.

                    CR 1973, Article by
                      Rev. P. O'Gallachair
                      The Rows are arranged from
                      South to North.

                        130

Kinawley Cemetery
Co. Fermanagh

To Michael MacKenna, d. 17 May 1884, aged 50
His wife, Catherine, d. 4 May 1916, aged 71.

CR 1956, Article by
Noel Maguire

St. Begnet's Church
Dalkey, Co. Dublin

Erected by Edward MacKenna in memory of his
beloved wife, Ellen MacKenna, who departed
this life 18th April 1850, aged 34 years.

"Success to the Farmer"
Tombstone of Toale MacKenna of Shig
Tydavnet Old Cemetery

APPENDIX V

MacKenna Pedigrees and Wills

The Origin of the MacKennas

Fiaca son of Niall of the Nine Hostages had four sons:
Eochaidh the Fair who hated the only-begotten (otherwise
Colgan) and Tuathal of the North from whom are Cenel
Fiachach of the North who belong to the Fir Leamhna,
Fothad the Madman, Aengus the Orphan. Eochaidh the Fair
had five sons: Oillil and Art the Younger and Fland of
the Plain and Dond of the Battles, and Cairpri who gave
his name to Magh Cenel Cairpri. They are extinct. Maine
Munchain from whom descend Cenel Maine in Cenel Fiachach.

Another party says that those five are sons of Daimin of
the Silver Face and that he in turn is a son of Colgan.
The party also says that Daimin's name belongs to Tuathal
of the North and that he is the fourth Daimin among the
Fir Leamhna. And it is from them that the Sil Tuathail
of the North in Clogher of the grandsons of Daimin is
called.

The Book of Ballymote
83 b (1-21)

Eochaid the Fair who hated the only-begotten, for
which reason he is called Calcan had five sons:
Ailill, Art the Younger, and Fland of the Plain
and Dond of the Battles and Cairpri who gave his
name to Magh Cenel Cairpri and whose seed does not
survive today. Maine Munchain son of Eochaid the
Fair from whom are Cenel Maine are in the same
region, that is, in Cenel Fiachach. They were the
clan of Colcan son of Fiacha.

The scholars say that Daimin, that is, of the Silver
Face was a son of Calcan and that he was the father
of these five men and that party also says that the
name belongs to Tuathal and that he was the one
with the seven sons, that is, the seven sons of
Daimin among the Fir Leamhna. And his name was
Daimin and it is his seed who make up the Sil
Tuathail in Clogher of the sons of Daimin today.

The Book of Lecan
61a:41-61b:2

Translation by
Dr. Joseph Duffy
Bishop of Clogher

132

The Cenel Fiachach Mic Neill

The Race of Fiacha Son of Niall
(of the Nine Hostages)

870. Fiacha son of Neill of the Nine Hostages for whom was
bestowed four sons and three daughters. The four sons
were: Eocha, the Fair One, with the unblemished face
otherwise referred to as Calgan. Tuathal of the North
as from him descended the stock (line) of Fiachach and
the men of Lemna in the North. Fothadh, men of
knowledge, the third son. Energetic Aenghus the fourth
son. The three daughters; Finnabair the wife of the
king of Cruachan; Rustic Temair wife of the king of
Leinster, dwelt in the plain of Cuinsitin. Aife of
Uisneach who was called wife of the Ulstermen from being
at one time in Ulster. There was also another daughter
by one of the sons by Aenghus, she was named versatile
Teine; she made a bridge of fire through which the steeds
were able to venture through, an incident which happened
one time in the Ormond region, that is, in O Shaughnessy's
territory. Those are, then, the three daughters of
Fiachach son of Neill.

871. Fair Eocha of fair features, who was known as Calgan,
had five sons: Oillil and Art (six children by him)
and Flann and Donn of the battles and Cairpre (after whom
is the Plain of the line of Cairpre); Maine Muncain son
of Echach the fair from whom is the stock of Maine of
the Fiachach stock (line). Thus listed are the children
of Calgan son of Fiachach.

872. Daimin, silverbrowed: it's said of him that he was a
fairy son of Calgan and Calgan father of the six was
the protector and the seven sons of Daimin with the men
of Lemna and Tuathal in the North and thus the progeny
of Tuathal came into contact with the household of
Daimhin.

873. The children of Oilell son of Calgan, the head; here are
their names: Mairne and Cianan, Conall and Fuatach with
whom was associated Mail in Kells and Conallan with
relatives in the region of Tulach and Cianain in Cashel
with relatives. The children of Mairne - they were
Conmain, Maelan and Bolcan.

874. The progeny of Floind (Flynn) by whom were Catmogha and
Coman.

875. The progeny of the fighting Duinn, that is, Bran and
Duinechaidh (Donogh) and Labhraid from whom was Tomaigh
and Lethfoda relatives with the Sinche family and Brain
with relatives under the leadership of Fiachach and
Duinechaidh of Ceall territory and of royal blood.

876. Four sons had Duinechaidh, that is, Oilill and Anmchadh,
Dunghaile and Laeghaire. Clan Dungaile in the country;
they were Dimusaigh and Cerbaill, Cein, Uainighe and
relations. Seven sons had Oilill and they all died
except the children of one son, that is, Oilellan in
the plain of Enaigh. Anmchad son of Duinechaidh had
three sons: they were, Mael Muaidh and Dunchadh and
Lorcan. Mael Muaidh had two sons, they were Tirechan
and Uallochan. Lorcan had two sons Cian and Laegaire.
Dunchad had two sons: Mael of the golden hair and
Mael Muadh. Mael Muadh also had two sons Lorcan and
Mael Morda from his the Lorcain and Mail clan.

877. Mael Mordha also had five sons: Duinechaid, Fergal,
Foilgni, the bright faced, Donn and Ruaidri (Rory).
Lorcan had one son, Mael Muadh from whom is Mhail
Mhuaidh, son of Lorcan.

878. Flann by whom is one son; Oilill the brave one. Oilill
had one son Cathusach. Cathusach had four sons, they
were Mithidhein and Ainiarrach, Eimhin and Aengus.
Mithidhein had seven sons and I'm not able to list them
but the family of two sons, Tadg and Cathal. Tadg had
two sons, Dubh and Adha. Adha had five sons, Flann,
Conn, Tadg, Find and Eiccertach. Cathal had one son
Buadhach. Buadhach had two sons, Dubh, the brilliant
one and Cairpre. Dubh had two sons, Tadg and Andruth.
Cairpre had two sons Flann and Buadach. Buadach had
three sons, Lorcan, Ruarc and Cairpre. Cairpre had
one son Buadach. One son for Buadach, Cathal. Three
sons of Cathal son of Buadach son of Cairpre, Mael
Ruanaigh and Giolla Dubh and Buadach.

879. The Ainiarrach clan, Ainiarraigh and Luinin and Flaitiusa.
Clan of Emin, the people of Caisil and the people of
Drom Soileach. Clan Aenghus, Murchadhan with relations.

880. The two sons of Tuathal from the North, the eminent
Amalgaidh and wild Conaing. These were noble septs
from them, the Indeirghe tribe with relations in the
port of Black pool (Dublin) and the Cosgraigh (Cosgrave)
tribe of the north and the Ciblechan tribe and the Emugan
tribe with their relations also. The two noble septs
which took over power were Gilla Munna son of Indeirghe
and Eochacan son of Cosgraigh and it is those who mainly
had power even though the rest also availed of it.

881. The progeny of Conaing whose children were numbered among the saints, Colman ale and Suanaigh and Colmcille and the bishop Aedha, The Clan of Lucht Telcha with whom was Colman ele, Eitigan and relations. The clan of Dun Cuirre from whom is Suanaigh, Braenain with relations. The progeny of Conaing from Brosnaigh to the North belonging to Colmcille but the Aemdha clan; they were Tresachan and Conaing noble from the O'Neills from Brosnaigh of the north, Eitigan; nobles of the O'Neills of Brosnaigh to the south. Cleirigh, Lachtnaig of whom is the Bishop Aedha.

Source - O'Clery Genealogies

p. 225

Patrick MacKenna   =
of Truagh

d. 11 May 11 Jas. I

   Niall MacKenna   Shane   Donel   Ross

p. 242

Tully oge MacKenna   =
of Derryclonard, Gent.

d. 10 Jul 1623

   James MacKenna

Patrick MacKenna   =
of Lower Truagh, Gent.

d. 10 Jun 1608

   Patrick MacKenna   Shane MacKenna
                                        1608

Neal MacKenna   =

Patrick MacKenna   =
of

d. 19 Sep. 1615

   Gillegroome

p. 243

Art MacKenna   =
of Neloone, Ballynemaskeragh

d. 9 May 1627

Dunslevy MacKenna

Patrick MacKenna   =
  of Dromullan
   d. 1603

      Toole

Gillegroome MacKenna =

Laghlan MacKenna   =
  of Killcoragh
   d. 1621

      Ross MacKenna

p. 244

   Manus MacKenna   =

   Gilduff MacKenna   =

   Phelim MacKenna   =
     of Mullaghcorras
      d. 20 Jan 1628

         Edmond Reagh MacKenna

   Phelim Carragh MacKenna =
     of Leckie
      d. 4 May 1620

         Ardill MacKenna

   Patrick MacNeale MacKenna =
     of Drumbristin
      d. 9 Nov 1616

         Dunslieve boy MacKenna

137

Cuconnaght MacKenna   =

Brian MacKenna   =
    of Ballintony
  d. 10 Feb 1628

    Brian MacKenna

Laghlin MacKenna   =

Patrick Boy MacKenna   =
    of Mollaghselsana?
  d. 10 Mar 1622

    Donal MacKenna

Toole Boy MacKenna   =

Neale MacKenna   =
    of Mullaghnacask
  d. 1 Jun 1629

    James MacKenna

Toole oge MacKenna   =
    of Carnaback
  d. 1 Jul 1622

    James MacKenna

Shane MacKenna   =

Patrick MacKenna   =

Neale MacKenna   =
 of Mullahabragh

 d. 1 Jul 1629

    Brian MacKenna

Donagh MacKenna   =
 of Rakely

 d. 10 Nov 1620

    Hugh MacKenna
    b. 1603

p. 248

    Shane MacKenna   =
     of Figullar, Derrylaffek, and Mullaghvad

     d. 20 May 1630

        Patrick MacKenna

    Shane MacKenna   =

    Patrick MacKenna   =

    Neale MacKenna   =
     of Mullaghnalan

     d. 10 May 1624

        Tully MacKenna
        b. 1599

p. 249

    Shane McGilpa Roe MacKenna   =

     d. 4 May 1628

        James MacKenna

Rory MacKenna   =

Patrick MacKenna   =
  of Cogabaska
  d. 12 Jan 1632

      Rory MacKenna

Hugh Carragh MacKenna =

Cormack MacKenna   =
  of Truagh
  d. 10 Jan 1632

      Owen   James   Cormack   Patrick

p. 250

  Shane MacKenna   =

  Owen oge MacKenna   =
    of Rossboy
    d. 1637

        Ross boy MacKenna

  Phelim MacKenna   =

  Tool MacKenna   =
    of Derrynamuck
    d. 22 Dec 1637

        Patrick MacKenna =
        d. before his father

  Ross MacKenna
    Heir to his grandfather
    b. 1622

140

p. 251

Melaghlin Duff MacKenna =

Owen MacKenna   =
 of Derrynallisk
 d. 1 Nov 1635

    Patrick MacKenna

Patrick MacKenna   =

Rory oge MacKenna   =
 of Lower Truagh
 d. 9 Apr 1637

    Patrick MacKenna
    b. 1626

    Source - Genealogical Office, Dublin Castle.

Pedigree of MacKenna of Raheny, Co. Dublin

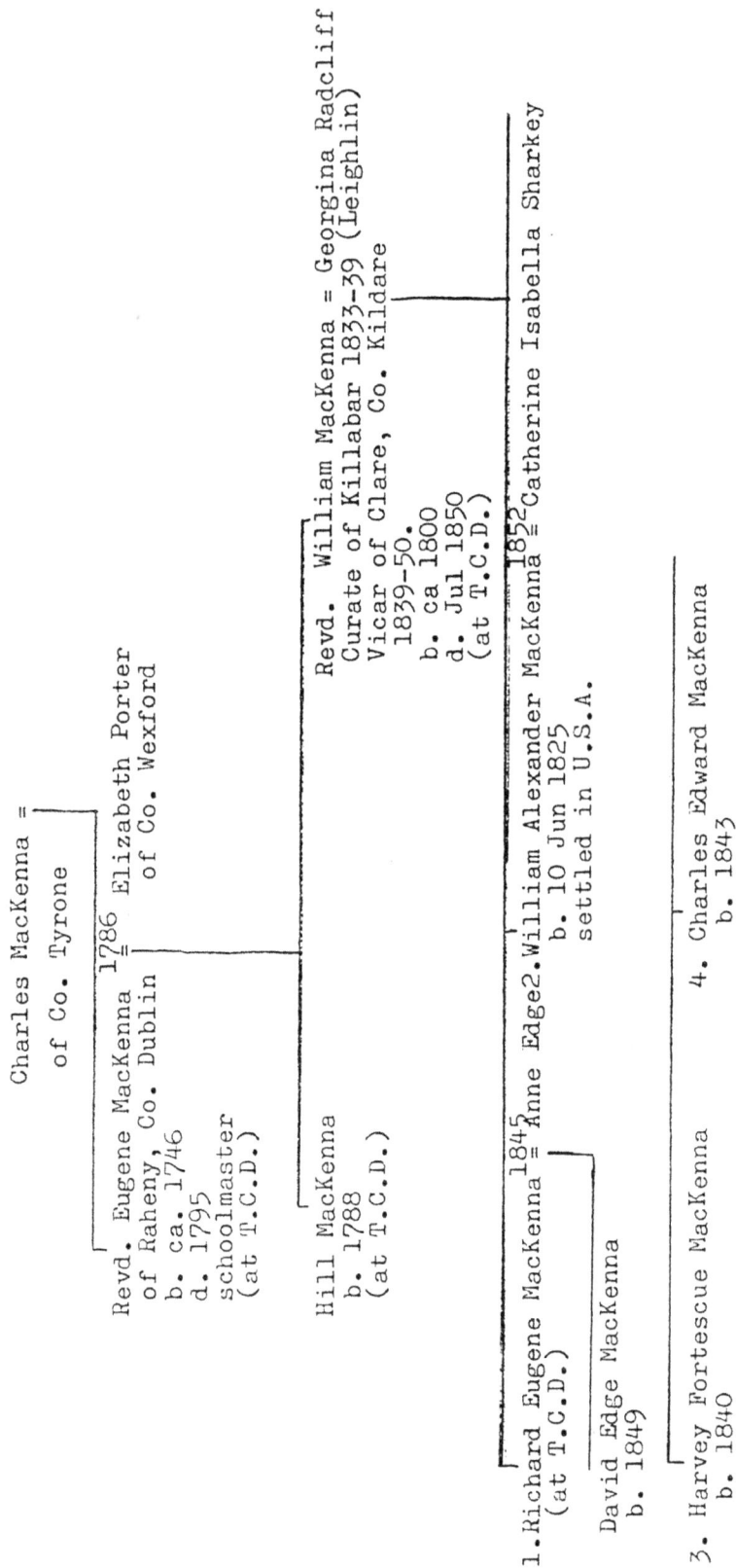

```
                    Charles MacKenna =
                     of Co. Tyrone    |
                                    1786 Elizabeth Porter
                                      = of Co. Wexford
                                      |
        ┌─────────────────────────────┴─────────────────────────────┐
Revd. Eugene MacKenna                                    Revd. William MacKenna = Georgina Radcliff
 of Raheny, Co. Dublin                                    Curate of Killabar 1833-39 (Leighlin)
 b. ca. 1746                                              Vicar of Clare, Co. Kildare
 d. 1795                                                  1839-50.
 schoolmaster                                             b. ca 1800
 (at T.C.D.)                                              d. Jul 1850
                                                          (at T.C.D.)

Hill MacKenna
 b. 1788
 (at T.C.D.)

                1845                                   1852
1.Richard Eugene MacKenna = Anne Edge  2.William Alexander MacKenna = Catherine Isabella Sharkey
 (at T.C.D.)                              b. 10 Jun 1825
          |                               settled in U.S.A.
David Edge MacKenna
 b. 1849

                                       3. Harvey Fortescue MacKenna    4. Charles Edward MacKenna
                                           b. 1840                         b. 1843
```

Genealogical Office Ms 819 (11)

142

MacKenna

Of Ardo House, Ardmore, County Waterford.

1. Owen MacKenna had:

2. Michael who lived a long time in Philadelphia, United States, America, and who had:

3. Michael, of Dublin (d. 1854), who had:

    I. Sir Joseph Neale MacKenna, of whom presently,

   II. William Columban, living in 1882.

4. Sir Joseph Neale MacKenna, M.P.: son of Michael; b. 1819 and living in 1887. Was twice m.: first, in 1842, to Esther Louisa (d. 1871), daughter of the late Edmond Howe, Esq., of Dublin; secondly, in 1880, to Amelia, daughter of G.K. Brooks, Esq., and widow of R.W. Hole, Esq. Residence in Ireland: Ardo House, Ardmore, co Waterford.

Source - <u>Who Was Who</u>. Vol. 1, 1897-1915.

<u>Burke's Landed Gentry of Ireland</u>.

MacKenna

Of Dundalk

1. Francis MacKenna of Monmurray: a grandson
of The MacKenna who, in March, 1689, was killed
while defending the Fort of Drumbanagher, for King
James II. Was twice married: first to Letitia
Adams; and secondly to a Miss Gernon. The children
of the first marriage were -- 1. William* or
"Big Billy;" 2. James, who settled in Philadelphia
early in life; 3. Felim or Felix; 4. Margaret, m.
to a Mr. Brennan. The said Francis MacKenna went
to Dundalk, and as above mentioned married secondly
a Miss Gernon of the county Louth, and became the
owner of an estate near Castlebellingham in that co.

2. John MacKenna of Dundalk: youngest son of
Francis; d. 1820.

3. William Alexander MacKenna of Dundalk,
solicitor: his son; m. in 1839, Ellen MacKenna,
his cousin, who d. 1849.

4. Philip MacKenna of Londonderry: his son;
living in 1882.

---

*William: This William (or "Big Billy") MacKenna of
Wilville near the town of Monaghan, who d. 1816, and
was buried in Donogh; married Ellen O'Reilly of
Ballymaurin, co. Longford, and by her had twenty-two
children, some of whom were--1. John MacKenna, a
general in the Spanish Service, d. 1814. (This John
being an officer in the Spanish Service inclines us
to believe that the pedigree of this family could be
found among the public records at Madrid, or Cadiz);
2. Philip, of Tobago, d. unm. in Bristol, about 1832;
3. Captain William, d. unm. in Chelsea, about 1843;
4. Francis, a merchant in Drogheda, who m. Mary Markey;
5. James, who d. 1843; 6. Christopher, who d. young;
and 7. a daughter Ellen, b. 1819. The aforesaid
William was buried in a grave under a stone which has
the following inscription:--"Here lyeth the Body of
Phelemy MacKenna deceased the 15th April, 1666." It
is the belief of some educated persons in that neigh-
borhood, that The MacKenna who was (as above-mentioned)
killed at Drumbanagher in 1689, was buried in the
same grave.

Some MacKenna Wills at the Public Record Office in Dublin

James MacKenna of Moneyrea, Co. Down	d. 2 Aug. 1856
John MacKenna of Dublin	d. 1839
James MacKenna of Co. Meath	d. 1781
Rev. Edmund MacKenna, P.P. of Slane Co. Meath	d. Mar. 1717
Mary MacKenna of Belfast	d. 24 Apr. 1857
Patrick MacKenna of Ballyhea, Co. Kerry	d. 14 Jan. 1839
Teresa MacKenna of Dublin	d. 2 Dec. 1890
Andrew MacKenna of Glaslough	d. 1756
Mary MacKenna of Stackallen	d. 7 Dec. 1813
John MacKenna of Belfast	d. 7 Sep. 1855
John MacKenna of Corlost, Co. Monaghan	d. 1746
Francis MacKenna of Dundalk	d. 1784
Mary MacKenna of Dundalk	d. 1797
John MacKenna of Dundalk	d. 1744
James MacKenna of Dundalk	d. 1794
John MacKenna, P.P. of Carrick on Suir	d. 1806
Bryan MacKenna of Cappoge, Co. Louth	d. 1792
Rev. William MacKenna, P.P. of Nobber, Co. Meath	d. 1813

APPENDIX W

Ballads and Poems
MacKenna of Truagh

Out from the stately Woods of Truagh, MacKenna
    rides at noon,

The sun shone brightly, not a cloud darkened the
    sky of June,

No eye had he for nature's charms, they don't
    annoy his brain,

As through the flowery vales he takes his way and
    never draws a rein.

Before him stand the tall grey towers of Glaslough's
    castle old,

It holds a treasure in its walls more dear to him
    than gold,

For in it dwells his own true love, that gentle
    young Maureen,

Whom he hopes, please God, will bless his home in
    the Woods of Truagh so green.

'I have come to look upon you, love, for tomorrow I
    must go,

With my brave Truagh men to Benburb, there to
    defend Owen Roe,

I have come to look upon your brow and hear your
    answer sweet,

As if in battle I should fall we never again shall
    meet.'

'Go forth my love my blessings go and smite the
    Saxon's sword,

When you come back I'll be your bride without
    another word.'

With fond embrace they bid adieu, as the sun
    went sinking down,

Behind the western wooded hills that o'er-look
    Glaslough Town.

MacKenna lightly mounts his steed at the twilight of
    the eve,
It leads him over Dava Hills and Truagh's green
    shady woods,
Tonight he meets his faithful men on the green hills
    of Tyrone,
To meet the army of the North, at Benburb, on
    their own.

And well O'Neil was pleased to meet these gallant
    mountaineers,
Who kept the Saxon wolves at bay round ancient
    Truagh for years.
Full well they fought on Benburb's plains, where
    England's flag went down,
And a few of them escaped that night towards
    Carrickfergus Town.

Oh! autumn winds being in the woods and berries
    ripe and red,
MacKenna and his youthful bride in Glaslough
    church were wed,
And never in his father's hall a fairer maid was
    seen,
Than MacMahon's only daughter, that gentle young
    Maureen.

            Courtesy of Peter MacKenna of New York

_____

The Battle of Benburb, 5 Jun 1646

Owen Roe O Neill, Commander of the Ulster forces
    during the Rising of 1641

CEIRTLE BHARRAIGH ABU!
— War Cry of the Mac Kennas.

THE MAC KENNAS OF TRUAGH

Accepted tradition is that Mac Kenna, a chieftain in Meath, being addicted to the chase, followed a stag of phenomenal endurance to Truagh where it was slain at Liskenna. He married a daughter of Treanor, Chieftain of Truagh, and this in time led to the installation of Mac Kennas as Chiefs of Truagh.

Their reign in Truagh (North Monaghan and South Tyrone) began around the 8th Century and during the ensuing centuries the Clan built up a fine reputation in all spheres of human endeavour. Their hospitality to Red Hugh O Donnell is recalled in "The Truagh Welcome". Their opposition to the plunder and confiscation of the lands of Ulster are equally well recorded in "The Green Woods of Truagh", etc.

The influence and control of the Clan in Truagh ended on 13th March, 1688, when they were defeated in battle at Drumbanagher, near Glaslough.

"A thousand times to tempt them to betray;
Life and rewards were offered them in vain;
They proudly cast the proffer'd boons away,
And spurned the tempter, with a cold disdain."
From "Death Before Dishonour"

mackenna

mackenna

"In omnem terram exivit sonus eorum" —
Their fame has gone forth to every land.
Motto of the Ultonia Brigade at Saragossa,
1st Nov., 1709, under Colonel John McKenna.

"McKenna lightly mounts his steed at the twilight of the eve.
It leads him over Dava Hills and Truagh's green shady woods.
Tonight he meets his faithful men on the green hills of Tyrone.
To meet the army of the North, at Benburb, on their own."
From "The Ballad of the Mac Kenna."

Ye waving woods of Truagh,
Once more I say adieu —
When far away in other lands,
My thoughts will turn to you.
And when my barque has run its course
Upon life's stormy sea,
Of early days and Truagh's green woods
My latest thoughts would be.
From "Mac Kenna's Farewell."

The surrounding Gaelic lettering was taken from the Deus on the front of the Clogher Cross, a reliquary of the late 13th or early 14th Century. It is appropriate since it coincides with a period of eminence of the Clan, it brings out the ecclesiastic involvement of members of the Clan, and the preponderance of the name in Clogher Parish today.

CLAN MAC KENNA

NAME ....

ADDRESS ....

....

....

....

Telephone Number: ....

Membership No. *100* ....

The Truagh Woods So Green

Excuse me good people, my talent's but feeble,
I cannot delate on the praise of Tyrone:
Yet part of that country where I am acquainted
To find out its equal I think there is none.
It's just and sincere they are, I declare,
In love and in friendship with me they have been,
And the fault was my own for leaving Tyrone
And returning again to the Truagh woods so green.

On the 12th day of May, it being a fine day,
In the year of Our Lord '64,
From fair Analoughan I straight took my way
Where twenty long years before I had been.
My friend, they all there, did vow and declare
That they were quite sorry to see me so keen
For leaving Tyrone, where foes I had none,
And returning again to the Truagh woods so green.

It was on that morning, bright Phoebus adorning,
Enchanting and charming was Dernaved hill,
With the blackbird and thursh in each bloomin' bush,
Might easily vie with sweet Philomel.
The linnet and lark in noble John's Park.
The buck and the doe are easily seen,
I pray don't exclaim, nor poor Hughes ever blame,
For returning again to the Truagh woods so green.

If you reconnoitre the verge of the county,
Where fair Favor Royal unfolds its demesne,
You'll find not in Erin, Scotia or Albion
Scenes half so charming or worthy of fame.
And loved Cavan Moutry I deem you the beauty
Of Erin, if I am not far overseen,
Where Minerva might rove in quest of the grove
That adorns the rest of the Truagh woods so green.

Farewell fond Tyrone, you're good men I own,
Which leaves me through life indebted to thee
Since you were so kind, it returns to my mind
To often revisit your beloved country.
But as my head's grey I'll do penance and pray
'Till called away some morning or noon.
I'll do my endeavour to gain the Lord's favour
In hopes to be welcome from Truagh woods so green.

If I were young and my learning quite strong
And my pen to be made of Illydian steel
I'd use all my might its praises to write,
For Truagh I could fight with sword and with shield.
It has lost its good name by the peoples own blame,
Yet I'm not ashamed the truth to unscreen.
If I were a poet the world would know it.
There's honour and truth in the Truagh woods so green.

To draw to a finish, why talk of the guineas
Some day I'd have hundreds if I'd stayed in Tyrone,
But I'm happy in mind, since God was so kind
Wouldn't I be ungrateful were I to make moan?
My sons they are made to that innocent trade
To handle the spade right manly and keen
And Favor Royal's sweet bell their hours does tell
As its echoes resound through Truagh woods so green.

- Composed by Patrick Hughes, Father of Archbishop John Hughes
of New York in 1764. Clogher Record 1964

Death of the Priest

I

A gray mist lay out on the mountain.
   And clung to the river below,
a sparkling of gold in the heavens
   framed Carrick Min Rock and Esh Roe
bold lashing rain slanted the valley
   and banged the white lake into foam.
When a horseman rode down in shadow.
   To tell us the priest had come home.

II

We feared not the stress of the weather.
   When tidings so joyfully were known;
the priest that was out on his keeping
   had ventured again to his own:
and Ellen below at the spinning.
   Struck up a sweet lilt of a song.
Tho' her voice, heaven rest her, was honey,
   my heart told me something was wrong.

III

At midnight came word to the village.
   That "Mass would be read in the glen."
The priest will be there with a blessing;
   Gold knows where he'll travel to then.
And Ellen and I went together
   right into the teeth of the wind.
And Paddy "Veel" Haimish, and Barney,
   and more I'm not able to mind.

IV

High up on Esh Mountains we listened.
   No sound but the wind in our ears;
it blinded my eyes tho' they challenged
   the thundering blizzard for years;
then down the wild glen-side we hurried
   to kneel on the damp heather sod.
And forward stepped Father MacKenna.
   The outlaw to worship his God.

V

And crowding to rude mountain altar.
   Were mountainy men by the score.
Tho hounded by the bloodhounds of England.
   The hindermost came to the fore
through the slush and the storm of December
   with often bog mud to the knee,
But wild as it was, when Mass started
   the night got as calm as could be.

VI

And there in the wild of the weather.
   I prayed as I never prayed before.
With Ellen contented beside me.
   In under my gray cota more:
the light on the altar was still as
   a sanctuary lamp in the shade.
And Father MacKenna the outlaw;
   bowed down to his Maker and prayed.

VII

And calmer the breath of the heavens,
   and softer the sound of the waves
the fragrance of summer came stealing
   from mountainy dungeon and cave.
But the red coats fast marching
   from Clogher.
Have rounded the hip of the hill
Sweet Savior, guard Father MacKenna
   they're after his reverance still.

VIII

We felt not the fate that was on us.
   We knew not the soldiers were there.
The good father turned with a blessing.
   His heart in the dream of a prayer.
He darkened the light came a thunder
   and flashed on the side of the glen
and the soldiers shot Father MacKenna
   God rest him in heaven Amen.

IX

We stole with the body between us.
　　The heretics chasing behind;
we lost them far down on the mountain.
　　And left them as fleet-as the wind
and back in the dawning of morning.
　　We rallied with slasher and spade.
And there on the sod where they
　　murdered him.
Father MacKenna was laid.

X

And one in our midst at the mourning.
　　Was said to have uttered a prayer.
Of revenge on that filthy Clann Luther
　　that breed of remorse and despair
and the one was Shane Bearna
　　the robber.
　　and Raparee　man of Slieve Beagh
when we ventured to chide him, the outlaw
　　was mounted and riding away.

XI

Bold Shane had revenge for he
　　followed the red coats to
　　Mahera Glen.
And he slaughtered the
　　murderers there.
　　With the help of his valorous men
but soon was the borderer taken,
　　betrayed for a handful of gold.

XII

And Ellen and I went together.
　　and knelt by the grave on the hill.
The altar was there to be sure. But
　　the mountain was lonesome and still
and I saw the tears wet on her lashes
　　but was she lamenting alone??
I saw him shot down, and I'm proud
　　that there may be were tears
　　on my own.

This event took place in a mountain glen in
Knockballyroney between Esh and Bragan. A monument
was erected in 1938 to the memory of Father MacKenna
who was shot here in 1754.

THE ROMANCE OF THE MERROW QUEEN

1

O'er Truagh's brown hills the day is breaking,
In Truagh's green woods the thrush is waking.
By Tully's lake the dawn is blushing,
Through Tully's bowers soft winds are rushing.
On Tully's shore a maid is moving.
And he who meets that maiden robing
Who may free his heart from loving.

2

Blue as the cloudless summer skies
Beams the soft lustre of her eyes,
White as the stainless winter's snow
Her neck and lovely bosom show
In massive curls of lightest brown,
E'en to the ground her hair floats down;
And around her tall and graceful form
A thousand budding beauties swarm.
So mildly gentle is her mien
She might be thought a village queen;
Did not her forehead broad and high
Proclaim her immortality.
And prove a soul was seated there
Too great for mortal frame to bear.

3

Now while the rosy morn awakes
His wonted walk MacKenna takes--
Conn Mac Art MacKenna Dubh,
Tiarna of the tribes of Truagh.
Tall in his form and grave his air,
Dark clustering hangs his raven hair.
Of fewer years no chieftain reigns
In Orghiall of the golden chains;
Yet in each line of brow and face
Deep thought has set its manly trace;
His thoughts are upon glories gone.
On warriors who in fight have shone.
How shall he, like those heroes, live,
Nor hostages nor tribute give?
What shall he do to make his name
Resound in song and live in fame?

4

He counts the deeds his fathers wrought,
The battle that those heroes fought,
And all the glories that have shone
Along the line of Heremon.

Since the three Collas in their might
Vanquished the race of Truagh in fight.
And conquered Orgiall of brown shields
In Acalethderg's bloody fields;
He pauses pondering o'er these deeds--
What moves amid Lough Tully's reeds?
He lifts his head and startled spies
The maiden with the soft blue eyes;
Alas that day he thought no more
On glory or on learned lore
For beauty seldom thought befriends,
And wisdom flies when love descends.

5

Deep lies in every heart the seed of love,
Unseen unknown, e'en to the parent bosom,
One breath alone its gale of spring can prove,
One sun of beauty bid it bud and blossom;
And when the sun that makes it summer, comes,
And beams upon the heart, till then reposing.
The germ of love at once buds forth and blooms.
Its myriad flowers and fragrance all disclosing
Love's germ for growth, nor days nor hours doth need,
For when the one sweet source of life is given
A lovely tree at once springs from love's seed--
And stretches its flower-laden arms to Heaven;
All joys the mind e'er dreamed about before
Bud forth upon this tree in loveliest seeming,
And he discovered joys ten thousand more,
Heart-flowers of love in love's sweet sunshine beaming;
Until the heart with joys and sweets opprest
Sinks fainting in the love-o'er-laden breast.

6

He drank long draughts of sweetness from her eyes,
With gentle love and tenderness o'erflowing
Like storm-raised seas his bosom heaves with sighs,
Upon his cheeks the deepening blush is glowing
His love hath reached at once full strength and size,
Warmed by the summer of that maiden's eyes.

7

Swift as the flash that lights the skies
Love's golden-headed arrow flies,
To shield the breast, to raise the pain,
To hide the wound, alike are vain;
Whom love thus wounds, he leads with chains,
And over his prostrate spirit reigns.
But when love thus triumphant rules,
In many an art his slave he schools,
He teaches from his wond'rous book,
The meaning of each tender look:

The ready tongue he oft denies,
But gives the language of the eyes
The secret hope the heart that heaves
Is written in love's magic leaves,
He shows what brings the lover's fear;
He traces to its fount the tear;
He tells why sudden blushes fly;
He reads the thoughts that swell the sigh;
Thus to his slaves does love impart
The language of the loving heart;
And never yet could fraud or pride
From Lover's eyes a true love hide.
In the same hour MacKenna found
At once love's wisdom and love's wound
From the fair maiden's eyes of blue
Love's learning and love's arrow flew;
Before her lips had love professed
Love's language had her love confessed;
The mantling blush upon her cheeks
Her passion's rising force bespeaks
The light that in her bright eyes glowed
The lovely maiden's heart-flame showed,
And all love's symbols plainly proved
MacKenna by the maid was loved.

8

"Daughter of beauty, white-armed maid,"
With faltering voice, MacKenna said,
"Whatever the cause that bade you bless
Triucha with your loveliness;
Whate'er the tribe from which you come,
Thrice welcome to MacKenna's home;
Bright shall that humble home appear.
If you will deign to rest you there;
The hundred hills you see around,
The thousand deer that o'er them bound;
The valleys with their forest green.
All, all, shall own you for their queen;
And every clansman that you meet
Shall bend like me before your feet."

9

Sweet as the shephard's pipe, from mountain ringing
Its music soft and clear,
And thoughts of home and absent loved ones bringing
To charm the wonderer's ear;
So soft, so sweet, so bird-like broke,
The maiden's words, while thus she spoke--

10

Dawn after dawn, when first the rising sun,
To ruby all my crystal lake is changing
From its clear depths I've watched thy footsteps, Conn,
As round my reedy shore thou hast been ranging;
Plain as the pebbles in the limpid brook,
I've seen thy mind upon its course careering;
For on the spirit's movements spirits look,
To their clear vision all its acts appearing.
Thought after thought, I've tracked across thy mind,
And, midst them all, not one of selfish feeling,
Or base or craven could I ever find
From the dark caverns of the spirit stealing;
But all sprang pure and spotless to my sight
Born of the love of fame and high achieving
In the rich panoply of glory dight,
And from thy soul the light of truth receiving;
I've sat and watched thee from my crystal bower,
The fountains of thy hopes and fears exploding
Until thy bosom seemed a beacon tower,
The light of honour all around thee pouring
And as each pure thought winged forth from thy breast,
I've wooed it to my own in rapt admiring,
As mortals prize the cast-off flower surpressed
To the fair bosoms their fond love inspiring
Until admiring deepened into love
And love to passion grew, both wildly proving,
That nought upon this earth may live and move
And keep its spirit free from blindly loving
And, now, although I be the Merrow Queen
I've lost my fairy power of self-concealing,
For love destroys the spirit's mystic screen
Its features to the loved one's eyes revealing;
Thus by the beauties of thy brave mind charmed
I stand, by love unveiled--subdued--disarmed.

11

So sweetly rose the maiden's words thus speaking
Her tale of love,
The thrush upon her mossy nest awaking
Forebore to move,
And listening breathless on her accents hung
Nor poured a note till her last tones had wrung.

12

As morn's first rose-light on the Memnon streaming
Wakes wond'rous music from the mystic stone,
So love's first dawn upon the young heart beaming
Brings forth the words that makes its passion known;
They come not of deep thought, or long preparing,
But from the love-struck soul, unbidden start
Like musk-winds a delicious odour bearing
Of joys that steep in (remainder of this line illegible)

13

And though the words of love be wildly spoken,
Faint murmuring from the lover's trembling lips
The heart that harkens to the tale thought broken,
Forgets them not, until its life's eclipse.
Close, and still closer, to the memory clinging,
They strangely mingle with the parting breath,
A strange wild rapture to the loved one bringing,
While struggling in the cold dark arms of death.

14

Faint murmuring thus, MacKenna spoke
Unbidden thus, love's accents broke;
The fond sweet tale of love he told,
Then new to him--but ah, how old;
The tale that tells of constancy,
From fear, from change, from doubting free,
Of tenderness that hourly grows--
Of fondness from the heart that flows--
Of fervent hope that flings its rays,
Like sunshine o'er the lover's days,
And makes sweet heart-flowers ever bloom
Around the lover's happy home--
The old, old tale that oft deceived,
And though deceiving, still believed.

15

She watched MacKenna when she spoke,
She marked each fond thought when it broke
From the dark caverns of his heart,
Like wild birds eager to depart;
She tracked each with her bright blue eyes,
As swift it mounted to the skies,
To find if aught impure or base;
Amid his fond love held a place;
And as each pure thought, stainless, rose,
High heaved with joy her breast of snows,
And rising rapture seemed to speak
In blushes from her changing cheek.

16

"Think not," with flashing eyes, she said
"Thou wooest now a village maid,
Who may be lightly won thy bride,
And then as lightly cast aside;
But since thy courage mounting high,
Would mate with one who may not die
Hear now the fate of those who dare
To wed the daughters of the air.
When spirits thus before love bend--
When from their orbits they descend--

When they forget their lineage high,
And wed with those who're doomed to die;
So long as in the mortal's breast
Unsullied lives the faith professed--
So long as love and truth there reign,
Undimmed by time, unsoiled by stain,
So long as earthly happiness
The faithful mortal shall possess;
Honor and wealth and fame and power
Shall be his high-born bride's rich dower;
No earthly joys shall equal theirs,
Unscathed by foes, undimmed by cares;
So long as earth's short life shall last
Defeat or woe he shall not taste.

17

"But if across their haven of love
One cloud of faithlessness shall move,
If but for once his heart should stray
Allured by other loves away;
Woe, woe, unheard of bitter woe,
Shall haunt him wheresoe'er he go;
Horror shall mark him for its own;
Despair shall make his heart its throne;
Dismay, defeat, a fameless grave,
On bloody field or yawning wave
Shall be the wretch's fate forlorn
Who weds with us and proves forsworn.

18

"Then pause upon this gulf's dark brink,
Lord of Triucha, pause and think
If the love-pledge thou now would'st take
Thy heart could ever wish to break;
If in thy soul thou now cans't see
One germ of foul inconstancy;
Turn thee, oh, turn thee now away
Let not this prove thy fateful day,
Nor from the Merrow's beauty trace
Dark ruin to thyself and race,
But if within thy constant soul,
Bright truth, unsullied, holds control;
If honour's shield thy faith defend;
If on thyself thou canst depend;
If the love-pledge, thy lips shall speak,
Nor absence, time, nor force can break;
If constancy can thus command,
MacKenna, take my heart and hand."

19

The pledge is given, the vow professed,
With all its dark denouncements laden;
The Merrow's clasped to his fond breast

159

His bride, his own, his peerless maiden;
For when did ardent love and youth,
Doubt their own constancy and truth,
Or think that o'er their passion's bloom,
A change or chill could ever come?

20

Around her feet upon the shore,
Its myriad buds the bog-bean bore;
White as the snow those buds then grew,
The lily's rivals in their hue;
But when the Merrow blushed consent,
As from the lake a bride she went,
That crimson blush, by some strange power,
Tinged with its hue the bog-bean's flower;
Reflected on the buds it fell
(Such is the tale Truagh's maidens tell).
So warm the blush, so bright its hue,
It dyed the young buds as they grew;
And from that hour the bog-bean shows,
Its young buds, rivals of the rose,
"The Merrow's blush" its gentle name
In memory of the Merrow's fame,
But the bright blush's tingling power,
Reached not the centre of the flower;
And when the blossoms wide unclose,
They still are tinted like the snows;
The lovely blush has passed away.
Like love before ambition's ray;
Or if its faint hues sometimes show
Amid the blossom's breast of snow
'Tis but as when the thoughts of love's first rosy bloom
'Mid age and care will sometimes o'er the bosom come.

21

But never in love's ceaseless right
Did loveliness or truth, or duty
More firmly bind his golden chain
Than did the Merrow's eyes of beauty.
Queen of MacKenna's conquered soul,
The Merrow ruled without control;
Each winged hour found her, as it passed,
Beloved more dearly than the last;
And love sat in his place of power,
Enthroned in Hi MacKenna's tower.

22

And with her came the promised dower,
Honour and wealth and fame and power;
Each year beheld his flocks increase,
And all the gifts of golden peace:
Two hundred steeds were in his stalls
Their riders thronged his castle halls;

His arm in battle still prevailed,
His foes before his war-cry qualied;
And e'en the Ardrigh of O'Neill
His friendship sought, and feared his steel.

23

'Twas vain to frame the subtle snare,
Or hidden ambush to prepare,
While by him sat the Merrow fair;
The whisper of approaching foes,
Would rouse her from her deep repose,
And she could reckon, from her bed,
Each coming footstep's iron tread.
Although Lough Neagh poured its floods
Between the foe and Truagh's green woods,
Then would she bid MacKenna rise,
While midnight ruled the dusky skies,
And to his listening ear relate
The foe's defying words of hate,
Their chiefs, their armour, and their plans
The names and number of the clans;
She could detect the ambuscade,
Though miles away in covert laid;
And tell the foes unguarded side,
And where to pour the battle tide;
Then would she gird him with her arms
And clasp him in her circling charms.
And fill him with a mystic might
That nought could stem in battle fight,
Some said such skill must magic prove
She said 'twas taught by mighty love.

24

But why ascribe to magic art
The brave deeds of the loving heart?
And why derive from magic power.
The goods that on the lover shower?
When love hath roused the sleeping soul
And dashed to earth sloth's dark control,
Then noble thoughts the lover move--
Then self is sacrificed to love--
Then will the thought of each loved charm
Nerve with a giant's force his arm;
Then will the hope to make her blest
Arouse the hero in his breast.
His strength will rise a thousand-fold,
Beyond the strength he used of old,
Because a thousand times more loved
Is she for whom that strength is proved.

161

'Twas in young spring's delightful hours,
When earth puts on her brightest dresses,
And decks her bosom with sweet flowers,
To greet the sun's renewed caresses,
Her husband sun, who from the south,
With all his bridegroom warmth returning,
Has kissed once more her balmy mouth,
And smiles away her wintry morning,
And fondly clasped her in his glowing arms,
And warmed to brighter bloom her ever-changing charms.

26

May-day is come, their bridal day.
The fifth that shed its happy ray;
Five years of love have swiftly fled,
Two sons have blessed their bridal bed,
Since first MacKenna wooed his bride,
Beside Lough Tully's silver tide.
The noontide meal is richly spread,
The guests are to their places led;
Kinsmen and kerns, a brave array,
Have met to grace the bridal day;
High at the board, the Merrow Queen,
All radiant in her charms is seen;
So winning is her noble grace,
Such sweetness breaths forth from her face
That chiefs and kerns who round her press,
Seem lighted by her loveliness.
His place beside, MacKenna takes
And as her sweet smile on him breaks
Joy lightens o'er the chieftain's eyes
Like sunlight o'er the dawning skies.

27

What fills the hall with wild surprise?
Why do the guests in wonder rise?
What flings aside the lofty door?
Who rushes up the sanded floor,
With flushing cheek and eyes of fire?
Hark, 'tis the herald of MacGuire;
And now before the chief he stands
With eager look and outstretched hands;
And loud before the clansmen all,
Thus rang his message through the hall.

"Lord of Triucha Cead Cladaigh,
The Saxon holds MacGuire at bay;
His land is in the foeman's power--
The brand is lit to fire his tower.
Haste to the rescue, haste away,
Lord of Triucha Cead Cladaigh."

29

MacKenna started from the board
And swiftly drew his flashing sword;
He grasped the bright sword by the blade,
His lips upon the hilt he laid,
Then 'mid his kerns and clansmen all,
Loud rang his answer through the hall.

30

"Now, by the Cross, the sign adored,
Traced on my valiant father's sword
I swear to meet the Saxon powers,
And die or free fair Tempo's towers.
I will not stoop beneath a roof,
Nor cool my long-maned courser's hoof,
Nor sleep nor taste of drink or food,
Until I drive the Saxn brood,
Like hunted wolves with steel and fire,
Far from the dwellings of MacGuire."

31

Grieved from the Merrow's side to part,
MacKenna clasped her to his heart;
Deep was the sigh that heaved her breast,
While fondly to his bosom pressed;
She thought she saw some form of dread
Half-hidden by the herald's head;
She strained her staring eyes to see
This vision of futurity.
In vain, the form was wildly passed
Like mist upon the northern blast:
She may not give a sign of fear,
When the chiefs and kerns are gathering near;
The wildering she may not breathe
That round her heart, like adders, wreathe.

32

"Colla da crich, aboo, aboo,
Arm, arm, and mount, my clansmen true;
Take down your bright arms from the walls--
Lead forth your strong steeds from their stalls--
Like arrow from the bended bow
To Tempo's leaguered towers we go;
Two hundred horse shall lead the way
And smite the foe 'ere set of day;
The kerns shall march on foot behind,
But horsemen should outstrip the wind."

33

Now side by side with rapid stride
In long array the horsemen ride
MacKenna moves forth in the van,
Tallest and bravest of his clan:
Past Muineachan's walls they speed;
Through fair Drumsnat they urge the steed;
O'er Cluaininnis's sainted ground,
The long-maned courser rushing bound;
And as 'mid Boylan's blue-eyed race,
The warriors pass with rapid pace,
Loud rose the friendly clan's hurrah--
"MacKenna, slainte geal go brath."

34

And now the Hi MacKenna go
Across the hills of Lisnaroe;
A lovelier prospect ne'er was seen
Than from those hills of emerald green.
Four lakes on one side brightly shone
Like diamonds flashing in the sun;
And on the other softly flowed
Wild wandering through the old oak wood,
The gentle river's silver stream
That glowed and sparkled 'neath the beam
And as it slowly moved along
Poured forth its peaceful undersong.

35

Westward the warriors hold their way
And seem to chase the flying day;
For now, his bright course nearly run,
Sinks in the western wave the sun,
And as his last rich beams he threw,
The towers of Tempo rose in view,
And seemed amid the setting blaze
Crowned with a coronet of rays.

36

Like leaves of the rose
The red clouds-close
Around the setting sun;
And violet hues
The East suffuse,
When day's last light has flown.
The twilight now falls
O'er Tempo's walls
With its mantle of soft grey
And a beauty shows
Of soft repose
More sweet than the glare of day.

Evening now rules with its gentle power
O'er Tempo's wood and Tempo's tower.

37

Now round its loved pines
The ivy twines
Its fondly clasping arms;
With mantle of green
It seeks to screen
Its consort from nightly storms.
Each flowerest first sips
With lovely lips
Its evening draught of dew;
And its leaves then close
In soft repose
Till sunbeams the day renew.
Day hath departed with heat and with light
And evening now leads in the sweet cloudless night.

38

Now dies the last ray
Of parted day
With light so cold and pale
All woodnotes are still
On vale and hill
Except from the nightingale.
Bright stars now appear
'Mid azure clear,
Out flashing, one by one:
And earth's verdant floor
Is silvered o'er
With beams of the crescent moon:
Moonbeams and starbeams now lend their mild light
To reveal soft charms of the sweet, cloudless night.

39

"Faire, Faire, now lash the steed,
Until his smoking flanks shall bleed;
Faire, Faire, now draw the brand,
And drive the Saxon from the land;
Sweep like a torrent on the foe--
MacKenna to the rescue,Ho."

40

As swollen rivers wildly gush
So fiercely now the horsemen rush
Like thunder peals the sound comes down,
Upon the beleaguered tower and town;
It seemed as if ten thousand men
Were rushing down the wooded glen.
The Saxon thought the Hi O'Neill
Were coming with their hosts of steel;

And quick withdrew their warlike powers
To Enniskillen's wave-washed towers.

41

The seige is raised, the foe is flown
The castle gates are open thrown;
Welcome, thrice welcome, to the friend
Who comes his kinsmen to defend--
Who with the speed of rushing storms
Has brought us safety with arms,
From hall, from tower, from young, from old
Within MacGuire's iron hold.
Rose, loud and shrill, the wild hurrah--
"MacKenna, slainte geal go brath."

42

Instead of battle fierce and red
The peaceful board is richly spread,
And at the board the highest place
Is given to brave MacKenna's race;
And close clasped hands and greeting kind
The ancient friendship closer bind;
Instead of wailing for the slain,
The harp now pours the joyful strain,
And as the wine cup passed along
Thus rose the bard's triumphant song:--

43

The Saxon came down with the sword and with fire
To waste and to slaughter the clans of MacGuire;
But he knew not when rushing with whoop and with hallo.
How true were the kinsmen of great Kinel Colla
Who comes, like a thunder-cloud driven by storms?
'Tis MacKenna, MacKenna, moving onward in arms.
Like broad-chested bloodhounds, his brave clansmen follow
Bringing safety and aid to besieged Kinel Colla
At the sound of his coming, the flash of his blade,
The Saxon fled hence to his fortress, dismayed;
And a kite and the eagle his dark footsteps follow
Pursued by the clansmen of brave Kinel Colla
Let white-bosomed Moira, the pearl of MacGuire,
Fill high for MacKenna the cup of desire;
Let her words, like the breathings of sweet music follow.
In thanks to MacKenna of brave Kinel Colla,
And long as the streams from dark Quilca descend
Let MacGuire to MacKenna prove brother and friend;
And with truth and with aid and with blessings still follow
The sons of MacKenna, of brave Kinel Colla.

44

The golden cup of Hi MacGuire
The cup of plenty and desire

Embossed and carved with art divine
Is now filled high with Spanish wine,
And placed by MacGuire's command
In his fair daughter, Moira's hand.

45

Fairest of all the white-armed maids
That bloom where Samer pours its water
Amid a thousand hills and glades
Is Moira, the MacGuire's loved daughter.
Her milk-white neck her hair enshrouds
In raven ringlets wildly flying.
Like masses of the inky clouds
Upon the snow-clad mountains lying;
Her smile that ever changing played
And as it plays new charms discloses,
A freehold for her dimples made
Of all her cheek's domain of roses;
And as when morning sunlight breaks,
Each hill-top with its lustre lightens,
So when the lovely maiden speaks,
Each face beneath her sweet smile brightens.

46

She bore the wine with swan-like grace
To where MacKenna held his place;
To her red lips she held it up,
Then to MacKenna gave the cup,
And thus while heaved her snowy breast,
The beauty-smitten chief addressed:--

47

"Colla da crich's most valiant son'
Branch of the tree of Heremon
Friend of my father, Conn MacArt,
Accept the thanks of Moira's heart;
When dangers lowered and foes assailed
And other friends proved false or quailed,
Faithful and fearless didst thou come,
To cheer, defend, and save our home--
Kinsman and friend, brave Conn MacArt,
Thy name shall live in Moira's heart."

48

Love wins the heart with many a wile,
But never does he so beguile,
As when he comes on friendship's smile:
When friendship speaks with beauty's tongue
Love ever blends its tones among;
But when warm thanks it fondly speaks--
When gratitude, like sunlight, breaks

167

Upon our souls from lovely eyes,
Love triumphs then in friendship's guise;
Such morn of friendship, sure and soon
Will brighten into love's hot noon;
The faithless beauty we may spurn,
The scornful beauty laugh to scorn;
But never, heart-free may we press
The hand of grateful loveliness;
Nor view, love free, the glance that flies
From grateful beauty's tearful eyes.

49

Upon the bowl his lips he laid,
Where woman's fingers last delayed;
He quaffed the wine and on its stream,
Her eyes warm glances seemed to beam.
He spoke of childhood's happy hours,
When first they met in Tempo's towers,
Of meetings warm, of words so kind,
(These should not pass like summer wind);
He praised each soft and mantling charm,
Which now bedecked her woman's form:
His lips by love and wine unsealed
His beauty smitten soul revealed;
He meant his words should kindness prove,
His heart betrayed him, and spoke love.

50

Low wailing as the banshee's cry,
Broke on his ear a long-drawn sigh;
'Tis strange none else perceives the sound
Nor comes it from the guests around,
Again its swells, so long and drear
His soul is smitten with strange fear.
He knows the voice--it cannot be--
She's far away--it is not she;
Again it sounds, like the death keen--
It is, it is the Merrow Queen.
Oh, false of heart; the night wind brings
The sighs thy falsehood from her wrongs.

51

MacKenna started to his feet,
And sprung upon his courser fleet;
The night is dark, with many a cloud,
The moon is wrapped in misty shroud;
Moonbeam and starbeam, both are gone,
The stream is deep, the way is long;
He cares not--onward, onward still,
He hurries over dale and hill.
The path is missed; the ford is lost;
How shall the swollen Finn be crossed?

168

See, where the foaming eddy swirls,
With spur and lash his steed he hurls;
From beetling rock he fearless leaps,
And sinks amid the frothing deeps:
The gallant steed now breasts the tide,
And gains unscathed the further side:
Away, away, like storm-clouds driven
By tempests o'er the face of heaven.
MacKenna flies to Tully's tower;
An age of woe seems every hour;
A weight of guilt sits on his breast,
With anxious agony oprest.

52

"If ere a day has passed away,
Since last in my embrace she lay,
I fling me at the Merrow's feet,
And pardon for my crime entreat--
It cannot, oh; it cannot be,
That she could bear to part from me."

53

Swift as the torrents headlong go
Adown the rocks of Assaroe,
When storms the rushing floods pursue,
Across the cataract of Hugh;
With such blind force and stormy haste,
MacKenna through the darkness passed.
His dark hair on the night wind flies,
The startled wolf before him hies,
And in the deepest forest cowers,
As if pursued by demon powers.

54

Now from Tighernach's shrine of Clones,
Ascend the midnight anthem tones;
From the grey Abbey's cloistered cells
The sound of peace and mercy swells,
But his heart's ceaseless throbbing drowned
The holy anthem's peaceful sound;
His soul with fear and grief distraught,
Nor sees, nor feels, nor hears of aught.

55

Away, away, by anguish driven
Like rack before the storms of heaven;
Although his mind no forethought hath,
His heart points out the shortest path,
By Donagh's lake he spurs his horse;
Through Drumsnat's glens he holds his course,
Past Muinlalban fast he flees.
At last, at last, amid the trees,
His own loved tower he dimly sees.

56

Who has not felt when first he sees his home,
After long time in distant regions straying,
Amid his rising joys a dark fear come
With icy hand upon his bosom weighing.
Do they still live? Thus asks the boding fear,
The loved ones whom your heart so fondly cherished
Shall their bright smiles your path of life still cheer,
Or have they in their bloom of beauty perished?
But when beyond this fear the wanderer knows
Himself against these loved ones an offender,
When, hour by hour, a giant horror grows,
That he himself has been a ruin sender,
A host of terrors o'er his bosom come,
Whene'er he lifts his eyes to that loved home.

57

The early lark now heavenward hies,
Morn's rose-light now is softly flushing;
It spreads its rich rays o'er the skies,
With light, and warmth and beauty blushing.
The little streamlets from the hills,
With spring's first crystal clearness gushing,
Flash back the rose-light from their rills,
And seem like streams of rubies rushing.
In loveliness the day-dreams break,
O'er Tully's hills and towers and lake.

58

He reins his steed, all clothed in foam,
And fondly gazes on his home:
The anguish, long his bosom's guest,
Now lighter sits upon his breast;
He lets his panting courser rest,
Upon his eyes his hand is pressed,
To cool his throbbing temple's glow,
And wipe the toil-drops from his brow;
His hand drops from his fevered eyes--
Why starts the chief in wild surprise?
What makes that sigh of anguish break?
Why flushes thus his pallid cheek?
He sees, he sees, upon the strand
The Merrow Queen before him stand.

59

The tears fall from her sunken eyes,
Her lip is faded by her sighs;
Pale as the marble is her cheek,
Down which the tears in torrents break;
She holds a child in either hand,
Beside her on the silver strand;
An ocean raised by sudden storms,
High heaves her bosom's snowy charms.

60

"Lord of Triucha--Conn Mac Art--
Chief of the weak and faithless heart,
Here, where we met we now must part;
I might have known thy earthly soul
Would soon disown love's pure control:
I should have thought before I placed
My hopes on one of birth debased,
How seldom truth and honour shoot
From an impure and worthless root;
But for the short and glorious hour,
When love o'er mortals holds full power,
They seem above base earth to rise,
And breath the words of Paradise;
Well may the spirit be forgiven,
Who takes them then for sons of heaven.
This dream is o'er--we here must part--
I speak not of my broken heart;
The words that suit weak mortal lips
I'll show the long and dark eclipse
Of hope, of mind, and energy.
The faithlessness has spread o'er me--
That deep heart-wringing endless woe,
Thy fleeting nature cannot know;
But all that human frame can bear,
Of misery and dark despair,
Of ruin to thy race and name,
Defeat, dismay and foulest shame,
Shall hunt thee to thy grave forlorn--
False--worthless--heartless--and forsworn."

61

"Oh, part not so, oh, part not so,"
MacKenna cried in bitter woe;
"Let misery and direst thrall
Fall on me--I deserve them all;
But say not that you love not me,
Spare me at least that agony:
See how my heart and soul repent,
Look how my mind with grief is rent.
Relent; oh, best beloved, relent,
This one--this only crime forgive;
Oh, say you love, and bid me live."

62

He raised his head to meet her eyes,
While heaved his breast with struggling sighs
He raised his head--but she has passed--
Those words of sorrow were her last;
For while he looks her pardon crave,
He sees her sinking in the wave;

171

And as she sank beneath the lake,
Loud sobs of sorrow from her break;
Within her lovely weeping eyes,
No shadow of dark anger lies;
But looks, and tears, and deep sighs show,
An agony of bitter woe
She took with her her children fair,
Twin darlings of the golden hair,
And left MacKenna--and despair.

63

When last was seen the Merrow Queen,
Soft spring had clothed the hills in green;
And ere the first rose bloomed in pride,
MacKenna by the Saxon died.
The autumn saw his castle fall,
Both lofty tower and banquet hall;
His lands were ta'en, his kinsmen slain,
Their skill was nought their courage vain.
A hunted herd, an outlawed race,
Their feet have known no resting place;
And from that hour, of all his clan,
There has not lived one landed man,
Such doom the Hi MacKenna prove,
For broken vows and slighted love.

"The Romance of the Merrow Queen" was written by
Hercules Ellis, the Clones poet, who lived about a
century ago. It is the longest and is considered by
many to be his best production. It relates to yet
another romantic and beautiful legend of the famous
MacKenna Clan and their dynasty of Truagh. The Merrow
Queen is the Mermaid Queen. The word merrow coming
from the Gaelic murdhuach or muruach.

Source:- The Northern Standard,
                July and August 1966.

Letter from Queen Elizabeth to the Earl of Tyrone

1592, July 26.--"Although at your last being here, we
did favourably, upon your humble submission, remit to you
a fault of no small moment in putting to death one of
the sons of Shan O'Neale without judgment by law, and
thereupon you did by special writing under your hand
promise to be a dutiful subject in living according to
our law, and to prosecute no action by force against
Tyrlogh Lenogh without complaint first made to our Deputy
and Council, yet we have been informed that hostility hath
been used by you against him, the cause thereof having
been since that tyme heard by our Deputy and some orders
taken betwixt him and you for observation of our peace,
which we will that both you shall observe, or else we
will not spare to cause either of you in whom the fault
shall be to be sharply corrected; but now of late hearing
of some other disorders lately committed, through you are
not personally charged therewith as the actor, yet the
circumstances are such as none may more conveniently
remedy the fault than yourself. The one is that the
breaking out of our castle of Dublin of Hugh Roo O'Donnell,
your son in law, and for whom you have been a long suitor
for his liberty and that you would be found for his good
behaviour. We understand that he hath not only taken upon
him the captenry of the country, his father living, but
hath made sundry raids upon Tyrlogh Lenogh's lands and
misused our sheriff in those parts. Whereupon as we perceive
from our Deputy the said Hugh O'Donnell, your son in law,
offereth to submit himself to such good orders as shall
become him to live like a good subject, nevertheless considering he is your son in law and in all men's opinions
dependeth upon you to be ruled, We cannot but earnestly
charge you, as you will have our favour, by which you know
how from your first beginning you have been maintained,
that you use your whole credit or rather your actual
service, as you shall be required, to reduce your said son
to his dutiful behaviour as our Deputy and council shall
require of him."

"A second matter also is very lately come to our
knowledge wherein none but yourself ought to give redress,
for about the 4th of this month, whilst the Lord Slane
and other our Commissioners were in the County of Monaghan,
the late country of MacMahon, to keep sessions, which they
did hold with the great liking of all the freeholders, your

son called Con did at the very day enter forcibly into the said country and the lands of Patrick MacKenna, and took a great prey and carried into Tyrone, to the dangerous example and nowise to be suffered unpunished. Wherefore, though we hope our Deputy hath not suffered the same to pass unpunished, yet we do charge you, that if by any escape of your son justice be not done, that you shall in your own person cause your son to be taken and delivered to our Deputy, and that full restitution be made to all the parties spoiled, or otherwise you shall cause us withdraw our former favours from you, which we would be very sorry to have occasion given by you."--1592, July 26.

Salisbury Ms. Pt. IV, 1892. Pp. 218-219.

Flax Flowers

APPENDIX X
MacKenna Landholders

MacKenna Freeholders in the 16th and 17th Centuries

Dunslive MacKenna, three tates - Rathkelly, Correneigh, Agherdrummuck

Owen MacMelaughlin MacKenna, one tate - Dyrretamych

Money MacKenna, one tate - Killyhomman

Ardell MacKenna, two tates - Kieltlevan (Killyslavin) and Tyrereen

Money MacGilduff MacKenna, one tate - Mullegudan

Patrick ponny MacGillerome MacKenna, three tates - Aghviclune, Dromcurrel and Dyrresoen

Patrick MacGillerome MacKenna, two tates - Killebyrne, and 2½ tates in Dirrery

Dunsleive MacKenna, three tates - Mullaghmyhenaght (Mullaghegny), Rathluam (Relaghan?) and Dyrrenevel (Derrnasell)

Nele MacKenna, four tates - Mullayhmore, Clonekyne (Clonkeen), Derreclone (Dernacloony) and Greighvassilogh

Toole MacKenna, one tate - Mullanekaska

Phally MacKenna, one tate - Ardegenny

James MacKenna, one tate - Nester, and two half tates of Killyloughvalley (Killyloughavoy)

Bryan MacKenna, two tates - called Tonaghes

Gilpatrick MacNele MacKenna, two tates - Drumbistie (Drumbriskin) and Glann (Glenbeg and Glenmore)

Phelim Carragh MacKenna, three tates - two of Balliveigh and one of Cullean

Brian Carragh MacKenna, one tate - Aghdrumcruer

175

Brian Balagh MacShane MacKenna, one tate - Shynneherne
   (Skinahergna)

Shane Ballagh MacKenna, one tate - Lissemvane

Brian MacEdmond Oge MacKenna, two tates - Kildryne and
   Toniomesk

Patrick MacMelaghlin MacKenna, two tates - Mullaghsneshonagh,
   and two half-tates of Mullaghmore

Edmond MacKenna, two tates - called Killerkie

Owen MacKenna, two tates - Durrenemuck (Dernamuck), and
   two half-tates of Knockhibin (Knockabane) and Drumlester

Dunsleive Oge MacKenna, two tates - called Aghevirrie
   (Aghadarra)

Art MacKenna, seven tates - Aghereske, Kills, Nevla,
   Balleneskragh, Aghesurd, Derevoy, and two half-tates of
   Killebrien and Coreclare

Tole Oge MacKenna, three tates - Dyrrenare, Luendengan, and
   two half-tates of Gillegullan, and Corgerleck

Tirlogh Duff MacKenna, three tates - Lesseagh, Derrelossad
   (Dernalusset) and Drumconragh (Drumcondra)

Gillegrome MacKenna, two tates - Killeberagh and Dirrehelan

Patrick Gillegrome MacKenna, two tates - called Kilmurry

Cormac MacKenna, one tate - Dougarbrie

Cuchonaght MacJames MacKenna, two tates - Ballinhown and
   Knockyrvan

Toal MacKenna, one tate - Dromcrall

Gildaff MacKenna, one tate - Killerane

Patrick MacNele MacKenna, one tate - Nasrishe (Astrish)

Cormac MacPatrick MacKenna, one tate - Killallon

Brian MacGromyn MacKenna, one tate - Dyrrenehinshe (Dernahinch)

Shane MacGilpa Roe MacKenna, one tate - Tonaghaamn (Tonnyfohanan)

176

Brian Boy MacOwen MacKenna, one tate - Kiltubret

Hugh MacShane MacKenna, one tate - Dromaddagan (Dunmadigan)

Tirlough Roe MacKenna, one tate - Kiltcrenan

Making in all about seventy tates
or about 4,200 acres.

Source - Survey and Allotment,
10 Nov. 1591 and subsequent
Inquisitions from MacKenna,
Parishes of Clogher, Vol. I.

MacKennas in the County Monaghan Inquisitions

Toll MacKenna, of Derreclonard, who owned three tates of
    180 acres, died July 10, 1623. James MacKenna, his
    son and heir, was then age 22 years, and married.
                            Monaghan Inq., 29 Oct. 1624

Patrick MacKenna, of Lower Truagh, owned three tates of
    land, which he transferred to Dunsleive MacKenna,
    without having obtained royal authority to do so.
    Dunsleive MacKenna entered on possession of them,
    and died January 10, 1608. Patrick MacKenna, his
    son and heir, was only 7 years of age. Neil MacKenna
    claimed 15/- per year out of these tates.
                            Monaghan Inq., 10 June 1625

This same Patrick MacKenna, of Lower Truagh, owned seven
    tates or 420 acres, which he made over on the 10 Dec.
    1608, to Edward Dowdell, Edward Shargold and George
    Hudson, in trust for himself, during his life, and after
    his death for his son, Shane MacKenna and his heirs.
    On the same date he transferred to the same trustees,
    five tates, for his own use during life, and after his
    death for the use of his son, Tole MacKenna, and his
    heirs. This Tole, when he came into possession of
    the property, sold three tates of it, without royal
    license, to Bartholomew Brett, of Drogheda. About the
    same time a John MacKenna, probably the Shane, brother
    of Tole, sold three tates to Thomas Blayney.
                            Monaghan Inq., 10 June 1625
                            Monaghan Inq., 10 Oct. 1626

Art MacKenna, who owned four tates, died May 9, 1626,
    Dunsleive MacKenna, his son and heir, was then 30 years
    of age and married.
                            Monaghan Inq., 25 Oct. 1627

Brian MacCuchonacht MacKenna, who owned, three tates, died
    February 10, 1628. His next-of-kin and heir, Brian
    MacKenna, being only 12 years of age, was unmarried
    on the 17 April 1629.

Neale MacTole MacKenna, died 1 June 1629, possessed of one
    tate. His son and heir, James MacNeale MacKenna, was
    then 7 years of age.
                            Monaghan Inq., 2 Oct. 1629

Neale MacShane MacPatrick MacKenna, who owned two and a half
    tates, died 1 July 1629. Brian MacNeale MacPatrick
    MacKenna, his son and heir, was then in his eleventh year.
                            Monaghan Inq., 2 Oct. 1629

Neale MacPatrick MacShane MacKenna, who died 10 May 1629,
owned four tates. Tolly (Toal) MacNeale MacKenna,
his son and heir, was then 30 years of age and married.
Monaghan Inq., 17 Sept. 1630

Dunsleive MacShane MacKenna, who owned two and a half tates,
died May 30, 1630. Patrick MacDunsleive MacKenna, his
son and heir, was then of full age and married.
Monaghan Inq., 17 Aug. 1630

Dunsleive MacOwen MacKenna, of Tawnagh, died 9 February 1627.
Owen MacDunsleive MacKenna, his son and heir, was then
20 years of age and married.
Monaghan Inq., 17 Aug. 1631

Cormac MacHugh Carragh MacKenna, who owned seven and three-
quarters tates, assigned six and a quarter tates to a
number of trustees, on the 8 August 1630 retaining in
his own hands only one and a half tates of Killyberrin.
He died on the 10 January 1632. Patrick MacCormac
MacKenna, his son and heir, was then of full age and
married.
Monaghan Inq., 20 March 1632

Patrick MacRory MacKenna, who owned a tate and a half,
died 12 January 1632. Rory MacKenna, his son and heir,
was then of full age and married.
Monaghan Inq., 20 March 1632

Owen MacMelaghlin Duff MacKenna, died November 1, 1635.
Patrick MacOwen MacMelaghlin Duff MacKenna was his son
and heir.
Monaghan Inq., 4 April 1636

Rory Oge MacPatrick MacKenna, of Killyhoman died 9 April 1637.
Patrick MacRory Oge MacKenna, his son and heir, was then
in his eleventh year.
Monaghan Inq., 28 Sept. 1637

Owen Oge MacShane MacKenna made over half his property in
Aghadarra, by deed in 1635, to his second son, Hugh
MacOwen Oge MacKenna. The said Owen died in 1637.
Ros Boy MacOwen Oge MacKenna, his son and heir, was
then of age and married.

Tole MacPhelmy MacKenna, of Dernamuck, on the 7 February 1629,
assigned his lands containing a tate and a half, to a
younger son, Phelim MacKenna. Tole died on the 22 Dec.
1637. Ros MacPatrick Oge MacTole MacKenna, son and
heir of Patrick MacKenna, the son and heir of the said
Tole, was then 15 years old.
Monaghan Inq., 10 Sept 1638

Laughlin MacDunne MacKenna, who owned two and a half tates,
    died May 8, 1639. Patrick MacKenna, his son and heir,
    was then of age and married.
                    Monaghan Inq., 12 Sept 1639

Patrick MacDunsleive MacKenna, on the 22 November 1629,
    assigned three tates of land to James Fleming, and
    Fleming assigned them to Robert Barclay.

Hugh MacMelaghlin MacKenna, died November 4, 1640. Laughlin
    MacKenna, his son and heir, was then 18 years of age
    and married.

Source - MacKenna, Parishes of Clogher, Vol. I.

MacKenna Proprietors in Errigal Truagh in 1640

Proprietors	Holdings	To Whom Allotted
Tool MacKenna Tirlagh MacKenna	Aghireske, Mullaghrien, Killoe, Derrycrinard, Mullen, 4 tates.	
Tirlagh MacKenna	Leseagh, 1 tate. Eloo, 1 tate.	
Shane MacTreanor Tool MacKenna	Derrivea, ½ tate. Derrivagh, alias Lisginive.	
Loghlin MacKenna	Killilaragh, 1 tate.	ANKETELL
Heirs of James Tool Oge MacKenna	Doonden, Killmegullen, 1½ tates.	
Patrick MacKenna	Corgarboy, 1 tate.	
Ardle MacKenna	Moygh, 1 tate, Killelekey, 1 tate.	
Heirs of Tool MacPhelim MacKenna	Derniamuck, Drumlaster.	MATTHEW
Shane MacKenna	Knockbeny.	
Heirs of Donagh MacKenna	Mullaghselsannagh.	
Donslevy MacKenna	Keffaghnione.	
Donslevy MacKenna	Dromfornesgye.	
Shane MacTreanor and Phelim MacEdmond MacKenna	Derrinerged.	
Bryan Oge MacKenna	Derrinevod, Ralvally, Mullaghmenagh, Tonagh, Mullaghnetony.	
Donslevy Boy MacKenna,	Drumdeston.	
James MacKenna	Mullaghetasgy	

Proprietors	Holdings	To Whom Allotted
Patrick Dunn MacKenna	Killihouran	Matthew Anketell
Patrick Groom MacKenna	Drummore, Drumartigan, Racally	
Gilligromme MacKenna	Aghwickkiline	
Tully MacKenna	Graghdrumsillagh	William Moore
Tully MacKenna	Clonkeene	Lord Massareen
Patrick Groom MacKenna	Luppan	William Moore Matthew Anketell
Garret Rooney & Phelim MacRedmond MacKenna	Mulliodum, Muliodum	William Moore Matthew Anketell
Tool MacKenna	Drumberrin	Lord Massareen
Patrick MacKenna	Coolebirne, Killebirne	Lord Massareen
Hugh MacKenna	Ballinahane	Simon Richardson Lord Massareen
Cormac Oge MacKenna	Mullaghneralag	Simon Richardson
Shane MacDonslevy Oge MacKenna	Killebrone, 1 tate	
Gillgromme MacKenna	Clunocullane	
Phelim Roe MacKenna*	Aghicurd, ½ tate, Drommemuckle, ½ tate, Killohiway, ½ tate.	
Phelim MacEdmond MacKenna*	Derrinerged, ½ tate.	
Hugh MacKenna*	Ballynahone, 2 tates.	

Source - Book of Distributions of the Down Survey from MacKenna,
Parishes of Clogher, Vol. I.

*Protestant land-owner

A List of MacKennas to Whom Premiums for Sowing Flax
Seed in the Year 1796 have been Adjudged by the Trustees of the
Linen Manufacture in County Tyrone

Aughalow Parish (Aghaloo)

Phelix MacKenna		4	wheels
Patrick	" Sr.	2	
Peter	"	2	
Barnaby	"	2	
William	"	2	
Samuel	"	1	
Terence	"	1	
Hugh	"	1	
Michael	"	1	
James	"	1	
Laurence	"	1	
Bryan	"	1	
Patrick	"	1	

Clogher Parish

Bernard MacKenna		2	wheels
Peter	"	2	
William	"	2	
Neal	"	2	
Michael	"	2	
Phelix	"	2	
Hugh	"	1	
Patrick	"	1	
Bernard	"	1	
Hugh	"	1	
Barny	"	1	
James	"	1	
Hugh	"	1	
Charles	"	1	

Argile Parish (Errigal?)

Ardel MacKenna	
Laurence	"
James	"
Patrick	"
John	"
Widow	"
Owen	"

Donaghedy Parish

Bryan MacKenna   1 wheel

Killeshal Parish (Killeeshil)

Denis MacKenna   1 wheel

Burndoney Parish (Badoney)

Hugh MacKenna   1 wheel

Termenmagurk Parish

(Termonmaguirk)

Owen MacKenna   1 wheel

Clonfecle Parish (Clonfeacle)

Arthur MacKenna   1 wheel

Arboe Parish (Ardboe)

Francis MacKenna

Source:- RIA Ms. 59-D24.

An Index to the Surnames of Householders Who Appear in the Tithe Applotment Books (1824-35) and Griffith's Primary Valuation of Ireland (1852-64)

MacKennas in County Monaghan

Baronies	1826 Tithe Books	1860 Griffith's	Parishes			
Truagh	T	332	Donagh	G	95	T
			Errigal Truagh	G	237	T
Monaghan	T	171	Tullycorbet	G	9	T
			Tehallan	G	9	T
			Tedavnet	G	106	T
			Monaghan	G	39	T
			Drumsnat			T
			Kilmore	G	4	T
			Clones	G	4	T
Dartree	T	38	Killeevan	G	13	T
			Ematris	G	1	
			Drummully	O		
			Currin	G	5	T
			Aghabog	G	9	T
			Clones	G	10	T
Cremorne	T	26	Tullycorbet	G	2	T
			Tehallan	G	1	T
			Muckno	O		T
			Clontibret	G	9	T
			Ballybay	G	3	
			Agnamullen	G	11	T
Farney	T	24	Magheross	G	1	T
			Magheracloone	G	1	T
			Killanny	G	5	T
			Inishkeen	G	7	T
			Donaghmoyne	G	10	T

MacKennas in County Tyrone

Baronies	1826 Tithe Books	1860 Griffith's	Parishes
Strabane Lower	None	10	----------
Strabane Upper	T	42	
Omagh West	None	1	
Omagh East	T	22	
Dungannon Upper	T	47	
Dungannon Middle	T	49	
Dungannon Lower	T	52	
Clogher	T	112	

T = at least one entry in the Tithe Books

184

APPENDIX Y

The Ballybetaghs of Truagh

The Ballybetaghs of the Barony of Truagh

If you have done any research into the old territorial division, you will know that an important division was the ballybetagh. Father James Smyth has a fine article on this in the Clogher Record in 1955.

In Father MacKenna's history of the Parish of Truagh you will find some references to the ballybetaghs of the Barony of Truagh largely taken from The Book of Inquisitions in Monaghan. There are many references to these also in Shirley's History of Monaghan with which you are no doubt familiar.

I had the privilege of examining Father MacKenna's manuscript from which he did Truagh Parish and I feel that he intended to outline the areas of the ballybetaghs but realized that it was a forbidding task, and somewhat irrelevant to the purpose of his main work. I decided that it was worth having a go at, and I did a rough map of the ballybetaghs of the barony (Truagh and Donagh). (See enclosed copy of the map.)

I am satisfied that the limits of the ballybetaghs in Donagh are reasonably accurate. With those of Truagh (parish) or Lower Truagh, I am not completely satisfied but at least it could be a basis for somebody else to work on. I believe I have accurately identified 'The 12 Tates' mentioned in MacKenna--also the church lands or termon lands which were the property of the Church of Errigal.

What set me off on this quest was the name of the district in which my school and the adjoining church is-- Ballyoisin or Ballyotion. Many had suggested that Ballyoisin was a ballybetagh. There is no townland or 'tate' of that name. But my school and the church, both in the townland of Knockconan are often referred to as Ballyoisin school and Ballyoisin Chapel. However, the townland of Knockconan is (as you will see from my map) in the ballybetagh of Ballaghareske which knocks that theory on the head.

I have arrived at a certain conclusion. On the map of the Down Survey of the barony there is named a tate called Killoe in the area of the present church and school. Cill =

Ballytoine

Bally-
Kiltlevan

Ballyveigh

Ballenegarva (Church lands of Errigal)

Ballaghereske

Ballykillmurry

The Twelve Tates

Bally-
Drombanagher

Bally-
Glaslough

Ballydavagh
(upper & lower)

Ballyclonard

Ballynesmore

Ballinlattin

Ballydromarrel

Ballyclonuoad

Ballylegacorry
or Ballichory

Termon Lands
(Church Lands of Donagh)

186

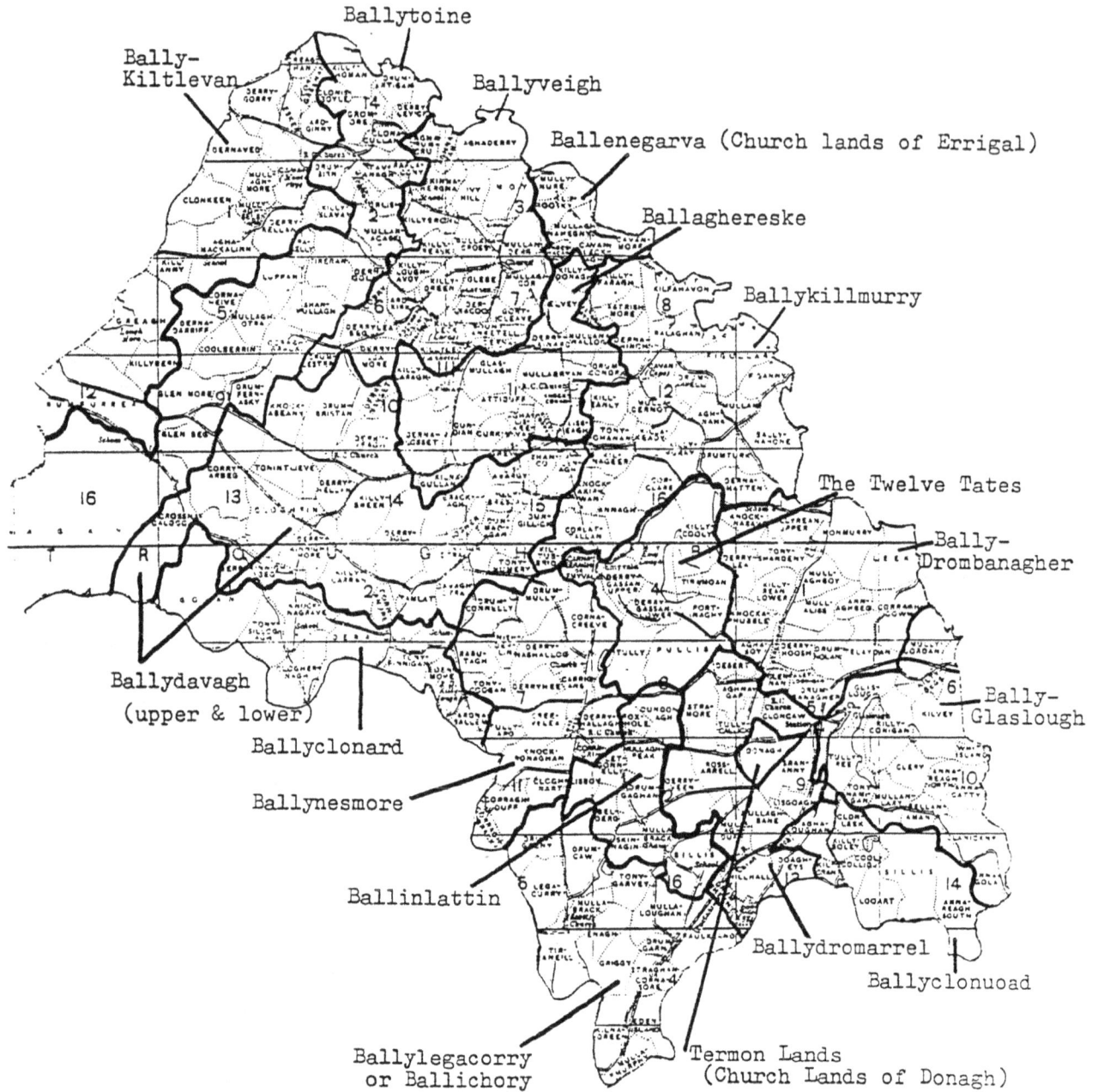

Courtesy of Owen Smyth
Based on the Ordnance
Survey Co. Monaghan
Townland Index, 1910.

church, eó = yew tree. A place where a small clump of yew
trees grew could be (according to Joyce) eónan or eotán or
eotin. The an or in is a diminutive suffix. I, therefore,
conclude that Knockconan is Cnoc Eónán (Hill of yews) and
that Ballyoisin is Bealach Eótain. Bealach = road,
meaning the road of (or passing) the clump of yews. This,
of course, is speculation but there is a scintilla of
evidence to support it.

To list the townlands of the barony and explain their
meaning is unnecessary as this was done about 140 years ago
by the eminent Irish scholar O'Donovan and his findings
are well reported in Shirley's History of Monaghan.

Father MacKenna has noted that many of the names of
townlands are derived from the names of trees that abounded
in the days of 'the green woods of Truagh.' A few simple
examples of this are:

 Killyslavan - Coillidh = (a wood)
      Sleamhain (the elm tree)

 Derrylavick - Doire (a clump of trees)
      Leamhog (the elm tree, another form)

 Dernahinch - Doire (as above)
      Uinnse (the ash tree)

 Derryhellan - Cuileann (the holly tree)

Among the townlands that Father MacKenna lists (and
quite a few are difficult to identify), there is one that
lost me many sleepless nights; the tate or townland of
Keffaghnione. Father MacKenna copies (correctly) this
list from the entry in the Book of Inquisitions. One must
remember that the recording of these legal proceedings in the
16th and 17th century was done in manuscript, very often
probably by clerks with a scant knowledge of the Irish
language and unfamiliar with the sounds of the Irish nomen-
clature. They were bound to make some mistakes. Later when
the manuscripts were printed in book form further occasional
mistakes were inevitable. The wonder is that mistakes were
not more numerous what with all the confusion of translating
evidence or statements often probably made or given in Irish
and written by hand in English or Latin.

Back to the townland I mentioned, Keffaghnione. There
is not and never was in Truagh a townland of that name.
It was just a few simple errors at one stage or other of the
recording process (I fancy at the printing stage) that gave us
a townland that didn't exist. When I remembered that the

early printed "S" looked like an "f" ($\int$), the rest was easy.
Here it is--Keffaghnione is really Kessaghmone which was
the name of the present townland Ivy Hill. (Father MacKenna
actually mentions this townland but gives it incorrectly
as Curraghmoin--I disagree with his translation also.)
I am convinced that the mone in the old name of this townland refers to the patron saint of Truagh St Muadain (or Mallon).
The Irish form would be pronounced Mone or Moan. It is significant that this townland is adjacent to the Saints' Old
Church "Errigal."

Source:- Owen Smyth

The Ballybetagh of Portclare

These townlands in the Barony of Clogher, County Tyrone were formerly part of the Parish of Errigal Truagh, County Monaghan. They were part of the ancient patrimony of the MacKennas of Truagh.

Altadavin Lower
Altadavin Upper
Cullamore
Derryclooney
Derryclay
Dernasell
Durless Black
Durless White
Drumadarragh
Fymore
Killaveney
Gallagh
Carrickavoy
Favour Royal

Source:- Dr. Joseph Duffy,
Bishop of Clogher

*   *   *

Places Where the MacKenna Chiefs Lived

Liskenna

Raflacony

Tully Lough   (on the crannog)

Tully   (in the ringed fort just above the
                  north eastern shore of the lough)

Innishdevlin   (near the Blue Bridge)

Portinaghy   (on the hill above Emy Lough)

Dernashallog

Emy Lough   (on the crannog)

Monmurry

Source:- McCluskey, Seamus.
Emyvale Sweet Emyvale.
1977.

189

AUGHER

Gallagh

Derry-
clay

Druma-
darragh

Fymore
Moutray

Fymore
Todd

Favour Royal Demesne

Eden
more

Killaveney

Durless
White

Durless
Black

Dernasell

Derry-
cloony

Altadaven

THE BARONY OF TRUAGH

COUNTY MONAGHAN

Carrick-
avoy

Cullamore

THE BALLYBETAGH OF PORTCLARE
Now in County Tyrone

190

APPENDIX Z

MacKenna Nicknames and Miscellaneous

MacKenna Nicknames

In 1835, John O'Donovan said that the MacKennas were amazingly numerous! They still are quite numerous. In 1977, there were 1,014 MacKenna voters in Co. Monaghan and 556 in neighboring Co. Tyrone. The authors of The Sign of the Stag tell us, "There are so many families of MacKenna around here that each group of related families has its own nickname . . . there are probably fifteen or sixteen hundred families of MacKenna in this area."

Nicknames are essential to distinguish one MacKenna family from another. Sometimes the surname is followed by the nickname (in brackets)--for example, James MacKenna (Owen). This form is more common in written communication. In spoken conversation the surname is skipped altogether and the person or family in question is referred to simply by the nickname--as an example, the Peter-Johnnies, the Art-Fedders, etc.

Owen Smyth, a native of Truagh has provided the following discussion on nicknames:-

There is the music of the names. You have met P.J. MacKenna (figuratively around Bragan nobody calls him Patrick Joseph MacKenna).

To the under twenties he is Packy Joe Pat John - to me and my generation he is Packy Joe Pat John Beag.[1]

His father was Packy Pat John.

His grandfather was Pat John Beag.

His great grandfather was John Beag probably to distinguish him from his neighbor or cousin John Mór.[2]

----

[1] Pronounced Beg (means small)

[2] Pronounced More (large)

N.B. I have given on right what would be the proper Gaelic or Irish forms of spelling. But nobody writes these. They are used only in speaking.

His neighbor in Crush (Crosnacaldo), Pat Treanor Phaidi[1] Bhig[2] died last year.

Down in Derryveagh (or Deravoy) lives James Phaidi Bhig.

In Golan (Parish of Donagh) there is Oweny Phara[3] Mhoir[4] and beside Knockconan School lives Malachy Para Mor (Treanor). But these are the simple ones.

A few years ago a ninety-year-old man was buried in Clara. He was Patrick MacKenna but the full handle was Patrick Peter Jemmy Pheadair[5] Airt.[6] It's interesting to note that the last two names are the Irish forms.

Back to Crush to the Mici[7] Fheilimi[8] and Jemmy Fheilimi families.

In one way you could say that the only MacKenna (or Treanor) in Truagh would be the priest if _he_ happened to be a MacKenna. All others got and accepted the nickname or the patronymic ad. infin. and it didn't bother them.

To list them all would be impossible. These are a few more: Peter Eoghaini[9] Paidi Ardail[10] in Killyslavan, James Eoghanai 'Mis[11] Eamuinn[12] in Drumbriston, Phara[13]

---

[1] Corruption of Padraig = Patrick (Pronounced Fadge-eh)

[2] Genitive of Beag (Pronounced vig)

[3] Corruption of Padraig (Pronounced Farah)

[4] Corruption of Mór (Pronounced Vore)

[5] Genitive of Peadar = Peter (Pronounced Fedd-ir)

[6] Genitive of Art = Art = Arthur (Pronounced id)

[7] Corruption of Micheál = Michael (Pronounced Mick-ee)

[8] Irish form of Felix (Pronounced El-emy)

[9] Corruption of Eoghan = Owen (Pronounced Oin-ee, O as in Loin)

[10] Irish form of Ardle

[11] Last syllable of Shéamais - same as Scots Hamish (Pronounced Mish)

[12] Irish form of Edward (Pronounced eem-on)

[13] Corruption of Padraig (Pronounced Farah)

Bharnai,[1] Pat Pheatsin,[2] Frainc[3] Tuathail,[4] Mici Tuathail, Neidi[5] Tuathail Sin[6] Og,[7] Phaidi Sheoin, Jemmy Sheoin, Eoghain[8] Sheonai,[9] Paidin[10] Phaidini,[11] etc.

This particular one struck my fancy. In the townland of Drumfernisky there is a MacKenna family nicknamed 'the Sailor.' As a boy I was told that some remote ancestor of theirs was a seaman. Later I discovered that at the confiscation of lands in Truagh following the Rebellion of 1641 the tate of Drumfernisky[12] was in possession of Donn[13] Selery[14] MacKenna and thus the origin of 'the Sailor' is purely Irish and is over 300 years old. I will explain later where the 'the' came from.

There is a section or group of the MacKenna clan, now mostly in Donagh Parish and Tydavnet Parish known as The Delaveys. This is a relic of what was once a very popular MacKenna name - Donnsleibhe[15] which if I remember rightly was the name of the father of Kenna, the founder of the clan.

---

[1] Irish form of Barney (Pronounced Varney)

[2] Corruption and diminutive of Pat (Pronounced Fat-sin)

[3] Frainc = Frank

[4] Irish form of Toal (Pronounced Toal)

[5] Neidi = Neddy

[6] A genitive of Sean = John (Pronounced Shin)

[7] Irish word = young (Pronounced og as in bog)

[8] Owen (Pronounced Oin) see 1.

[9] Corruption of Sean = John (Pronounced Yaw-nee)

[10] Corruption of Padraig and diminutive (Pronounced Pa-gin)

[11] Corruption of Padraig and diminutive (Pronounced Fad-nee)

[12] Drom or Drum = hill or ridge. Fernisky is a corruption of Fearnoige which is the gen. of fearuog - the Irish word for the alder tree. The name of the townland means the hill of the alder tree.

[13] Commonly used as part of Irish names. The word itself means the color brown - the wild bull was often brown and was referred to as the "Donn." e.g. The Donn of Cooley in the Cuchulainn saga. A man called Donn should be as brave as a brown bull.

[14] An English spelling of the Irish word Siollaire = of mighty blows.

[15] Donn = brown bull; Sleibhe = of the mountain. In the Book of Inquisitions the name is often corrupted as Dunslew.

It is worth remembering that the next door clan neighboring the MacKennas was the most powerful clan in Ulster--the O Neills of Tyrone and Armagh. Often the MacKennas were aligned with the O Neills in tribal or territorial squabbles, sometimes against them but in general the MacKennas acknowledged the sovereignty of the O Neills--in fact they had little option. Numerically they were inferior. This had its influence in the choice of names among the MacKennas. We often find Nial or Nealy MacKenna, also Hugh and Felemy, names which were popular with the O Neills.

All three of these have been fossilized in the local forms. In Truagh Parish there is an abundance of Nealy (MacKennas) of Hughie (MacKennas) and the afore-mentioned Mici Fheilimi and Jemmy Fheilimi. Most of the Hughes families in Truagh were MacKennas who adopted the patronymic as a surname--also a few MacAvins from the Latin form of Owen (Eoghan) which was Oviin.

There are also families (of both Treanors and MacKennas) known as Harley, derives from Searlat--which is but an Irish form of the English Charley or Charles.

MacMeel or MacElmeel also abound in Truagh but this is a Co. Fermanagh clan as pointed out clearly by Dr. P. Mulligan (Bishop of Clogher) in an article in the Clogher Record.

The ancestor of a MacKenna family in the Clara district was called Pat the Boy and his progeny are known as James the Boy, etc. This is a corruption of Paidi[1] Buí which literally means Yellow Paddy. The Irish word Buí, meaning yellow was in this area pronounced 'boy,' but as the meaning of the Irish form ceased to be understood in an English speaking community it became Pat the Boy. The Buí (boy) probably referred to the prevalent hair coloring.

A red haired person was called Rua (pronounced Roe) and so we get John Roe, Peter Roe, etc.

The Kellys and MacCuskers of the Ballyoisin district were probably transplant tenants by a landlord called Cope

---

[1] The Paidi became 'Pat the'

194

who also had large estates in Co. Tyrone in the Fintona
area where these names abound who through marriage with a
landed lady came into possession of several townlands
or tates in the Ballyoisin district of Truagh parish.
Cope's name still lives in a townland called Cavan-Cope.
The Pat Veals and the John Veals have their origin in
'Mhichil' the genitive of the Irish Micheál = Michael.

The Sheam (as in Seam) MacKennas are from an abbre-
viation of Seámus, locally pronounced Shee-mas, the Irish
form of James.

Another popular O Neill name Seán (pronounced Shane)
gives the Phaidi Sheáin (s) (pronounced Kane (s)) and
another genitive Shinn (pronounced Kin) combined with
Hugh (pronounced - U) gives us the family Kin-oo.

It's all a fascinating subject and deserves a book
on its own.

Source:- Owen Smyth

195

Glossary

Gillegroome -   the gloomy youth or grim youth, from gruamdha.

Aghy (Oghy) -   from the name of the horse god.

Glasny - (Glaisne)   from glasnach meaning green.

Moder (Modera, Modartha) -   a nickname meaning grim.

Tigearna (Tiarna) -   lord as in Lord of Truagh.

Termon -   a sanctuary.

Creidiong -   trustworthy, respectable, believing.

Braonlios -   a fortress near a water flow or drop.

Abhonlios -   a river fortress.

Ponny -   from pana meaning awkward or untidy.

Phally -   A pet name, failidh (faili) meaning cheerful, hospitable or welcome.

Monny -   possibly monach, full of tricks or guileful or from mongach, a lot of hair or long-maned.

Mac Over -   Iver? possibly ower meaning pale brown or dun colored.

Mac Tevoll -   Teimheal, meaning darkness, dark or obscure.

Niall Gus -   Gus denotes vigor or gusto, the chosen one.

Triucha Ced -   a territorial division which began as a unit of military organization. It means the 150th part of the island (Ireland), because it was the 30th part of a Cuigead, i.e., a fifth or province.

The Triucha Ced contained 30 ballybetaghs (baile biataigh). Ballybetagh means the townland of the victualler or steward. This steward was a public officer whose duties were to supply the king's household with provisions, to furnish necessaries for the army, and to provide entertainment for travellers.

The steward was required to entertain the
chief and his soldiers when on the march in
the 'betagh' direction. For this purpose,
the steward was endowed with the ballybetagh
which he held rent free. Professor Hogan
thinks the ballybetagh "may be regarded as
originating in the subdivision of the population group; which each supplied its quota of
fighting men."

*   *   *

MacKennas in Foreign Military Service

Spain

(MacKenna) MacKana, Juan, Cadete, 1724

> Source:- Wall, Richard.
> "Irish Officers in the
> Spanish Service: II.
> The Regiment of Limerick."
> in·The Irish Genealogist,
> 1977, 1978, p. 604.

MacKanagh, Don Estevan,	Lieut.	1721.	Dragones de Edinburgo.
MacKanagh, Don Juan,	Lieut.	1768.	Regimento de Hibernia.
MacKenna, Don Juan,	Sub-Capt.	1724.	Regimento de Limerick.
MacKenna, Don Juan,	Adjutant.	1761.	
Don Juan,	Sgt. Maj.	1762.	
Don Juan,	Lt. Col.	1761.	
Don Juan,	Col.	1777.	Regimento de Ultonia.

France

MacKenna, Col. 1868.

This officer was so dangerously wounded in the Battle of
Reichshoffen that he had to resign the command of his
regiment, The 2nd Regiment of Cuirassiers. "A heroic charge
by the French cuirassiers at Reichshoffen did little more
than create a great legend, of troopers plunging to death
in the hop-fields with a futile courage worthy of the
countrymen of the Knights of Crecy and Agincourt."

> Source:- Brogan, D.W. France Under
> The Republic. N.Y.:
> Harper, 1940.

Various MacKenna References

A.D. 1592, <u>Barony of Farney</u>, <u>Co. Monaghan</u> Brian MacShane MacKenna[1]

1601, <u>Barony of Farney</u>, <u>Co. Monaghan</u> Mullaghlin MacPatrick MacKenna[2]

1641, Among those who supported MacKenna in the Rising of 1641: Owen MacCormac MacKenna and Patrick Punny MacKenna

1666, <u>Dreagh</u>, <u>Parish of Magheracross</u>, <u>Co. Tyrone</u> Patrick MacKeane[3]

1689+ <u>Parish of Magheracloone</u>, <u>Co. Tyrone</u>, Toole Boy MacKenna of Magheracloone outlawed by Williamites[4]

1719, <u>Bath Estate</u>, <u>Barony of Farney</u>, <u>Co. Monaghan</u> Cohana MacKana[5] - Garranroe alias Cornemuckle, and Drumheriffe - 219 acres.

1790-1811 <u>Story Estate</u>, <u>Clogher</u>, <u>Co. Tyrone</u>

Paddy MacKenna[6]
Johnny MacKenna (1792)
Neddy MacKenna (1795)
Alice MacKenna, Terence MacKenna, Frank MacKenna (1807)
Owen Creena MacKenna at Taminacrin
John MacKenna (1790)
Charles MacKenna (1790)
Jim MacKenna (1796)

1797-1837 <u>Fintona</u>, <u>Co. Tyrone</u>

J. MacKenna taught at hedge school No. 22[7]

1827, <u>Mulnacross</u>, <u>Parish of Drumsnat</u>, <u>Co. Monaghan</u> Charles MacKenna - 2 acres, 2 roods[8]

---

[1]Clogher Record, 1955, p. 124

[2]Clogher Record, 1956, p. 110.

[3]Clogher Record, 1953, p. 10.

[4]Clogher Record, 1967, p. 366.

[5]Clogher Record, 1967, p. 344.

[6]Clogher Record, 1970, pp.245-246.

[7]Clogher Record, 1971, p. 497.

[8]Clogher Record, 1966, p. 73.

1861, <u>Tullycaghny</u>, <u>Parish of Muckno</u>, <u>Co. Monaghan</u>
<u>Charles MacKenna - house</u>[1]

Noteworthy MacKennas:

Donogh Roe MacKenna of Maghera, Co. Derry, O'Donovan called him "the best Irish Scholar in the North," (in the Gaelic oral tradition). Donogh Roe was 91-years-old when he provided information to O'Donovan in 1834. The MacKennas of Maghera had gone north from Monaghan during the time of the 1641 Rising.

*   *   *

Bibliography

McCluskey, Seamus. <u>Emyvale Sweet Emyvale</u>, 1977

Téllez-Yáñez, Raúl. <u>El General Juan MacKenna</u>. Buenos
    Aires: Editorial Francisco De Aguirre, S.A.,
    1976.

MacKenna, J. E., MacKenna, J. R. and MacKenna, P. A.
    <u>The Sign of the Stag; A Chimera</u>. Rumford, Me:
    Rumford Publishing Company, 1973.

---

[1] <u>Clogher Record</u>, 1966, p. 183.

AFTERWORD

I cannot think of a more satisfying way to conclude this
study of the MacKennas of Truagh than by bringing to your
attention a wonderful organization that has been created to
preserve the MacKenna heritage. I speak of the Clann MacKenna.
In March of 1980 a group of those interested in the MacKenna
heritage met at the home of Mary McKenna, Kilrudden House, in
Clogher, Co. Tyrone. This meeting led to the creation of a clann
society. In April 1990, due to the efforts of Mary McKenna and
Plunkett McKenna, the clann was reformed and great
accomplishments have been made steadily ever since.

Some of the goals of the Clann MacKenna are to: study and
promote the use of ancestral names; record tales, songs, stories
and traditions; restore the old cemeteries; mark out a MacKenna
heritage trail; produce an annual journal; and to create a coat
of arms for the society.

Highlights of the past two years include: a reunion in
November 1990 at the 4 Seasons Hotel in Monaghan; a MacKenna
float featuring the 'hunt' scene which won a Community Trophy in
the Heritage Year St. Patrick's Day Parade; a second Annual
General Meeting in April 1991; the publication of the first issue
of the *Clann MacKenna Journal* in 1991; and a gathering in 1991
which featured a tour of places of historical interest in
Monaghan and Tyrone with traditional music, song and dance in the
evening.

Plans for 1992 include a clan rally in Monaghan on 22, 23
and 24 May followed by participation in a national gathering of
nearly 100 clans at Tara of the Kings in Co. Meath.

If you would like to join the Clann MacKenna and receive the
excellent *Clann MacKenna Journal* here are two key addresses:

Orders for journal and membership dues to:

    Maria McKenna, Registrar   £6 in Ireland & Europe
    Clann MacKenna   £7 elsewhere
    Derrykennighmore   £10 for libraries
    Emyvale
    Co. Monaghan
    IRELAND

Articles, news, reviews to:

    Sean MacCinna, Hon. Editor
    Clann MacKenna Journal
    1 Old Armagh Road
    Monaghan
    Co. Monaghan
    IRELAND